Holidays and Holy Days

Susan E. Richardson

DEDICATION

To my mother, Martha Richardson,
for all those trips to the library when I was growing up,
and,
to my father, Marvin Richardson,
for teaching me that when you want to know
something, look it up.

CONTENTS

BEFORE WE BEGIN. . .

The book you're holding is one I wished for many times over the years I worked in a Christian bookstore. Customers came in asking about holiday customs or how a holiday got started, and I had nothing to answer their questions. I wrote this book to answer those questions as well as I could.

During my research, I discovered that many questions don't have a specific answer. Christians have been arguing about what holidays – if any – we should celebrate and how to celebrate them since Christianity began.

For example, in A.D. 245 an early church leader, Origen, wrote that it was sinful even to consider celebrating Jesus' birthday "as though He were a King Pharaoh." Later Christians in Armenia and Syria accused Roman Christians of sun worship for celebrating Christmas on December 25th.

During the fourth century, Augustine of Hippo stated, "we hold this day holy, not like the pagans because of the birth of the sun, but because of him who made it." Then Pope Gregory I sent Augustine of Canterbury to England in A.D. 596 as a missionary, instructing him to observe the people's customs, giving old traditions Christian meaning to help spread the faith, "for from obdurate minds it is impossible to cut off everything at once."

Two hundred years later, in 742, Pope Zacharius reversed Gregory's decree and sent out an edict prohibiting Christians from participating "in heathenish customs of the season." The discussion still goes on today as people learn the origins of various holiday customs. Some believe that Christians should abandon customs with roots in pagan celebrations while others believe that the current meaning of the custom is what is important, not the origin.

I don't plan to take sides in this or any argument. As these different pre-Christian celebrations come into the text, along with church decrees for or against various traditions, I'll present them without drawing any conclusions. What the origins of our customs mean to Christian holiday celebrations is – I believe – for you as an individual to decide with the guidance of the Holy Spirit.

As you read, you will also notice the repetition of "probably," "perhaps," and "may have," rather than positive statements of fact. Researchers can trace few customs with any degree of certainty. Some traditions may have logical sounding explanations but no hard evidence to prove them.

Two other pieces of information included may need some explanation. First is the information at the beginning of each month's section about the birthstone and flower for each month. Though some background for birthstones goes back to the zodiac and superstition,

Christians do use birthstone themed gifts, including on products available in Christian stores. I included the material to answer another commonly asked question and add value to the book for the purchaser.

The other is the information on Jewish holidays. Because Christianity comes from Jewish roots, and many Christians are curious about what these holidays mean, I have chosen to include brief sections on them. Hopefully, this will also make the book more useful as a reference tool, though the information does not include full details on current celebrations.

I hope you will consider time with this book to have been well spent and enlightening.

No one can write a book like this without a lot of help. Without the encouragement, suggestions, and support of Angie Hunt this book might never have gone from a dream into reality. Angie, I know I've said it before, but I'll say it again: thank you! You always have the answer when I have questions.

Terri Blackstock has my profound gratitude for her prayers, support, and friendship over the years, not just while writing this book. No one could ask for a better sister and brother in Christ than she and her husband, Ken.

Pamela Brown and Ann Jacobson, my readers, have my appreciation for plowing through an early draft, giving me suggestions and comments on the content, then still being willing to look at an extra chapter.

Kay Emery, retired from DaySpring Cards, and Jim Hauskey of DaySpring Cards made my section on Clergy Appreciation Day possible by putting me in touch with others, sending me information, and offering suggestions on that section. Jerry Frear of Under His Wing and Dan Davidson of Focus on the Family provided the remaining information on Clergy Appreciate Day.

Thanks, too, to Deborah Keener of the Wayne County Public Library for responding to an email request for help, and then moving my query to the top of the stack when my schedule moved up.

I would be remiss in this new edition if I failed to thank everyone at Servant Publishing who made my first publishing experience an enjoyable one. Kathy Deering, I appreciate your kindness through the process and your patience as an editor with a brand new author. Everyone at Servant was unfailingly kind and helpful.

Thanks are also due to the people at Regal Books, who bought Servant's backlist when Servant disbanded. Their graciousness and generosity to those of us who had works acquired in the process is without peer. Kim Bangs, I still say that you write the nicest, most encouraging rejection letters I've ever received!

Many thanks, too, to Kimberley Gardener Graham for working with me on the cover design. Kimberley, you've been a pleasure to work with as a client. Thank you for your kindness and help when the roles switched! I appreciate you not stopping until you got the cover to be the best it could be.

So many other friends have contributed over time. Suzanne Bailey, another client who's become a friend, is always willing to chop my words apart and make me stretch for something better. I'm a stronger writer because of your comments.

My niece, Suzanne Catlin, also gives me great feedback and suggestions when I need them. You'll always be in my heart.

I appreciate my friend, Jan Clifton, for her prayer support and honest responses to my work when needed. You make my life better just by being my friend.

And finally, in the words of Paul: "Thanks be to God for his inexpressible gift!" 2 Corinthians 9:15.

HOLIDAYS AND
HOLY DAYS

Blessed are those whose way is blameless, who walk in the law of the LORD! Psalm 119:1

Holiday celebrations have existed as long as humans have. Over the years, people have celebrated seasons, life changes, and divine beings. Maybe we have a God-given need to mark special days and events. After all, God used celebrations and feasts to mark special days for the Jewish people. He also designed them to foreshadow Jesus' coming.

We get the word *holiday* from a blend of *holy day*. Early in history, all holidays were holy days, whether Christian or pagan. Christianity was not born into a vacuum. Our faith came into a world where customs already existed.

Jewish customs provided the foundation for Christianity. Jesus was born into a Jewish family and lived a traditional Jewish life throughout His earthly ministry. Scripture tells us that He observed the feasts and holy days of Judaism. Not only did He attend worship in synagogues, He did much of His teaching there.

Since God designed the Jewish celebrations to point to Jesus as Messiah, Jewish customs and holy days were a natural part of newer Christian celebrations. Most of the first Christians were Jews. This quickly changed as Christianity grew.

Jesus had commanded that Christianity not be restricted to Jews.

1

The apostles went beyond the Jewish community to win converts. Wherever they went, new Christians came to faith with a pre-existing set of ideas and customs.

Church history tells us that the early Christians opposed anything contrary to the gospel. Many people chose to die rather than to worship the emperors of Rome as gods. If they saw a custom as pagan, they refused to take part in it.

They saw other customs as harmless or immediately gave them new meanings. Sometimes, old customs became a part of Christian worship when the former pagan beliefs no longer seemed to be a threat. However, various customs not necessarily contrary to Christianity seem to have crept in over the years.

Thanks to the roads provided by the Roman Empire, missionary efforts spread further across the globe. Each new culture added more customs. The church sanctioned some of these additions. Others simply refused to die out.

In America, a unique set of circumstances arose. Immigrants from around the world settled in the new country, bringing together a variety of customs and traditions for the first time. As America grew and changed, ethnic groups traded different traditions. English, Scotch, Irish, German, and other national backgrounds lived in a common land with a new common identity as Americans.

As a result, holiday celebrations in America became multi-cultural affairs. Along the way, they have also changed from holy days to holidays. Religious tradition doesn't have a connection with some holidays. Others may have begun as religious observances but now have added different elements from other sources.

This leaves the modern Christian with many questions. Why do we do the things we do? Which parts are from Christian tradition and which from other sources? The profile of each holiday or holy day will attempt to answer these questions.

Birthstones

Over the years, different groups designated a flower and a gemstone as the official representative for each month. Birthstones appear on nearly everything, not just jewelry. Most people view these gems and flowers as a matter of custom or fun rather than superstition, so they will be included in each month throughout the year. You'll find them listed on each month's page throughout the book.

The idea of a specific stone belonging to a particular month has been around for centuries, though the stones have varied through the years. Some say the idea began with the twelve stones in the High Priest's breastplate. Others linked them with the twelve signs of the zodiac. Each birthstone supposedly brings either powers and virtues or misfortune to influence a person throughout the year.

The modern list of stones has more to do with business sense than with superstition. In 1912 the American National Retail Jewelers' Association adopted the current list of stones at its convention. Before the list's adoption, jewelers had used various older lists. Without a commonly accepted list of gems, jewelers could not recommend a particular stone knowing that the recipient would understand the significance. Also, some of the stones on these lists were either difficult to obtain or were currently out of fashion, making sales more difficult.

Using older lists based on the zodiac complicated matters further. The signs of the zodiac predated the Roman calendar, so many of the signs covered parts of two different months. In creating their calendar, the jewelers looked at how much of a month was in a particular sign, and the gem associated with the longest amount of time became the birthstone for that month.

For example, the sign of Scorpio runs from October 23 to November 21. The traditional stone for Scorpio was topaz. Since most of November is in this sign, the birthstone for November became topaz. In addition to a stone for each month, they gave an alternate stone for five months: March, June, August, October, and December.

Today the changes continue. Using November as an example again, newer lists often show citrine as the appropriate stone instead of topaz. In this case the change probably results from the popularity of blue topaz. More people thought of blue instead of the traditional yellow with topaz. Switching to citrine keeps the color consistent.

Church History - A Very Brief Glimpse

As you look at many holidays, you'll find many began in the "Eastern" Church or the "Western" church. These may make more sense if we start with a brief look at how the early church grew. You can find much of the early history in the book of Acts. After the portions of history recorded in Scripture, centers of faith grew in several places. Gradually people referred to these centers by location: in the East or in the West.

For the first part of Christian history, Jerusalem was the center of the church. From there the apostles first went out to spread the gospel. Antioch, where people first used the term Christian for followers of Christ, also developed as a center for the young church. Other centers grew in Alexandria in Egypt, Byzantium - otherwise known as Constantinople - and Istanbul in modern Turkey.

Since these centers were close to where Christianity began, we can trace many early observances of Christian holy days to the Eastern church. Over time, the gradual rise of Roman Catholicism made the Western church important in setting celebrations. Catholic missionaries in Europe and America won many converts. When Rome accepted a holy day, all Catholics accepted it, too. The more people who looked to Rome for leadership, the more Rome set what holy days people observed.

Other parts of the West shared leadership with Rome. Centers in Carthage (North Africa), Toledo (Spain) and Tours (western Europe) influenced church direction. Monasteries in Britain and Ireland grew to have great power and influence as well. All of these added to traditions the Western church accepted.

Unfortunately, East and West often disagreed over what holy days Christians should celebrate and when they should celebrate them. Even today, you'll find differences remaining. We'll look only at the historical differences.

Beyond the division between the East and the West, the Protestant Reformation brought another breach to the church. As with the previous division, the Reformation changed both customs and holy days. Since the Reformation will come up later, here are a few basics to help you.

If you know a little about church history already, you probably think of Martin Luther when you think of the Protestant Reformation. He is, undoubtedly, the best known of the Reformers, but he wasn't alone. Other people in various parts of Europe wrote calling for reforms within the Catholic Church at the same time Luther wrote in Germany.

Luther's idea of reformation had nothing to do with forming a new denomination. He wrote against issues like selling indulgences, corruption within the church, and theological matters. The Lutheran church today takes its name from those who followed his interpretation of Scripture.

Because Luther was conservative in his reforms, the Lutheran church services looked much like Catholic services. He simplified the liturgy and included new music, but the biggest change was that Lutheran pastors preached a different theology. They emphasized personal redemption through grace rather than a works-based salvation.

Few customs, or normally observed holy days, changed, though Luther discouraged the idea of praying to the saints and observing saints' days. We'll see how this played into the history of Santa Claus later. Beyond that, the Lutheran church still celebrated the same holy days as the Catholic Church.

About the same time Luther was writing about the need for reformation in Germany, Huldrych Zwingli preached reformation in nearby Switzerland. The two differed in their focus. While Luther was concerned with purifying the church from its excesses, Zwingli believed that any forms of worship not specifically mentioned in Scripture were in error.

Zwingli's leadership resulted in a drastic change in worship. His followers removed all paintings, pictures, and statues from churches. They abandoned the old liturgy and holy days, and replaced hymns with psalms. Services in the resulting Reformed churches looked different from the older forms of worship. Even today, people can recognize Swiss Reformed churches by the weathervane on the steeple instead of a cross.

Similar reforms took place elsewhere, with the result that some holy day celebrations mentioned later might not be familiar to you if you belong to a non-liturgical church. If Scripture did not specifically mention holy days, reformers discarded them along with other parts of Catholic worship.

The English Reformation took place over a longer period of time. King Henry VIII started the process when he took over the leadership of the English church from the Pope. Later Edward VI continued the reform along the lines of the Swiss Reformation.

Elizabeth I came to the throne as a Protestant. Her tolerance allowed groups like the Puritans to practice their more austere style of Christianity. The growth of the Puritans, in turn, led to the English Civil War in the seventeenth century and the Commonwealth years under the rule of Oliver Cromwell, a Puritan.

As with other reforms, the changes in England affected various customs and holy day celebrations that appear later. The Church of England (Anglican Church) remained liturgical, following the basic liturgical year, while other denominations abandoned the liturgy along with other practices.

The history of your own denomination explains why some customs may or may not be familiar to you. We all inherit the decisions those who came before us in faith made about customs.

TELLING TIME

So teach us to number our days that we may get a heart of wisdom. Psalm 90:12.

You might think that New Year's Eve and New Year's Day are the logical holidays with which to begin. However, before we can look at how we celebrate the New Year, let's look at a year and the calendar's origin. For most of history, people celebrated the coming of a new year at the vernal equinox, the time in spring when day and night are of equal length. People usually celebrated on March 25th, though the actual date can vary somewhat.

So who came up with the idea of January 1 starting the New Year? The Romans first used January 1st as New Year's Day in 153 B.C. Though this was the first time for the change, people used varied dates for the New Year until Julius Caesar officially reformed the calendar much later in 45 B.C.

He based the new calendar on the Egyptian solar calendar with a few changes. The Egyptian calendar's months all had 30 days, with the extra five days tacked on at the end of the year as a festival. Julius Caesar spread the extra five days throughout the year. The Julian calendar also established leap year as occurring every four years, though the term did not come into use until later.

People called the year before the new calendar began, 46 B.C., the "Year of Confusion." To make the seasons match the month to start the new calendar the next year, Caesar lengthened and manipulated 46 B.C. The year had 445 days by the time it ended. In addition to the ordinary months, it had the month of *Mercedonius*, lasting 23 days, plus a 33 day *UnDecember* and a 34 day *Duodecember*.

As a reward for Caesar's work, the Roman senate renamed his

birth month, *Quintilis*, July in his honor. Later the senate gave his grandnephew, the Emperor Augustus, a similar reward when he corrected a mistake that had crept in. Those in charge of calculating leap year misread the edict, and had observed leap year every three years instead of every four years. They renamed the month of *Sextilis* August for his efforts in standardizing this and correcting the problems already present.

The calendar change created a few other problems as well. The names September, October, November, and December simply mean the seventh, eighth, ninth, and tenth months. When the calendar changed so that the New Year began on January 1st instead of March 25th, the names no longer fit.

For a time succeeding emperors gave them new names. September became *Germanicus*, *Antonius* and *Tacitus*, while November's names varied from *Domitianus* and *Faustinus* to *Romanus*. People found the constant changes as confusing as the wrong names and eventually the old, though incorrect, names, stuck.

Despite Caesar's efforts, after the fall of the Roman Empire and the rise of Christian nations in Europe, most countries returned to considering March 25th as New Year's Day. Then, in 1582, Pope Gregory XIII made the reforms which established our present method of calculating and dividing the year. At his proclamation, Catholics in Europe immediately adopted the revised calendar.

Protestants in Europe, however, were in the midst of the Reformation, when people viewed with suspicion anything vaguely connected with the Pope. As a result, acceptance of the new Gregorian calendar took longer. The Protestant portions of Germany finally adopted it in 1700. Great Britain, including the American colonies, did so in 1752, and Sweden in 1753.

Other parts of the world, such as the Oriental countries, considered it the "Christian calendar," but eventually adopted it as well. Japan began using the new calendar in 1873, and China in 1912. Russia actually adopted it twice, first in 1918, then again in 1940 after trying various other calendars.

The Gregorian calendar came to America before Great Britain adopted it. The Dutch settlers, as well as Swedes and other European immigrants already used the Gregorian calendar. In New England some groups such as the Quakers used the calendar but renamed the months and days to remove pagan associations. They became simply "First Month" or "First Day," and on through to the end.

The Roman word *kalends* or *calends* became our modern word *calendar*. To the Romans the word meant the first day of the month and the new moon, since the two originally coincided. The Christian custom of measuring years from the birth of Christ didn't begin until

A.D. 550. A Roman monk named Dionysius Exiguus worked out the method. People through the years have changed older dates to coincide with modern usage.

Weeks

We're so used to the seven day week that you may find it hard to think of other possibilities. The Egyptians had ten days in their weeks while the Assyrian week was six days long. Before they changed the calendar, the Roman week had eight days.

We get our current seven day week from two different sources. The Babylonians thought the moon took seven days for each of its four phases. Their calendar based a month on the moon's cycle, so dividing the month into four seven day week cycles made sense.

The second source for the seven day week is the Bible and Jewish tradition. God created the earth in six days, resting on the seventh and setting the pattern for us to follow.

The names of the days of the week come from Old English. Sunday and Monday go back to a Babylonian idea that a planet ruled each day. They considered the sun and moon to be planets also, so the sun's day and the moon's day were included. The remainder of the names comes from a variety of gods and goddesses.

Sunday The sun's day, from *sunnan daeg*.

Monday The moon's day, from *mona daeg*.

Tuesday Tiw's day, named for the Saxon god Tiw, son of Woden (Odin).

Wednesday Woden's day, from *wodnesdaeg*. People considered Woden the wisest of the gods and revered him as the creator god.

Thursday Thor's day. Some thought Thor to be a son of Woden. Others said that he was an older and more powerful god. The Normans called him Thur.

Friday Frigga or Friga's day. Friga was the wife of Woden and the goddess of married love.

Saturday Saturn's day, from *saeterdaeg*.

Sunday Worship

From the Roman "sun's day" how did we as Christians arrive at Sunday as a day of worship? Jewish people worshiped on Saturday, the Sabbath. In early Christianity, many Jewish believers still kept the Sabbath. Because Jesus rose on a Sunday, early believers considered it the obvious choice for Christian worship.

Keeping both was a simple matter. According to the Jewish method of reckoning time, the Sabbath ended at sundown Saturday and then Sunday began. By waiting until after sunset, they were able to move from Sabbath to the following "Lord's Day" easily. Doing so allowed the Jewish traditions and Christian worship to blend, with the Lord's Supper becoming part of the traditional Sabbath meal at the end of the Sabbath day. Jewish believers included their new faith in the traditional prayers of thanksgiving and praise, adding distributing bread and wine as Christ commanded.

Not long after the end of the first century, celebrating the Eucharist or Lord's Supper moved from the Sabbath meal to early Sunday morning before dawn. We have two possible explanations for the change. First was early persecution. Jewish leaders forced believers out of the synagogues, so they began to meet in private homes. Emperor Trajan had also forbidden "suspicious" gatherings in the evening. Moving the time to just before dawn removed problems associated with the decree and provided a practical solution, too. Sunday was an ordinary work day, so believers had to worship before going to work.

Second, more and more Gentiles were joining the church. Since they had no Jewish heritage, they did not observe the Sabbath prior to the Lord's Day. This led to problems within the young church, as the apostles had to decide whether or not Gentiles had to follow Jewish customs. You can read the discussion found in Acts 15. Throughout the New Testament, you can find other hints of disagreement between Jewish Christians and Gentile Christians as the two groups struggled to understand just what their common faith meant.

While Sunday worship was universal, keeping the Sabbath varied from group to group until near the end of the second century, when Gentile Christians became interested in the Sabbath.

When Emperor Constantine relieved the church from persecution A.D. 313, the hour changed from pre-dawn to 9:00 a.m., the hour Romans set aside for important business. Later, on March 3, 321, Constantine forbade unnecessary work on Sunday. This put the Christian day of worship on an equal footing with non-Christian assemblies and made it easier for believers to gather. His decree allowed Christian soldiers to attend services while serving.

Many churches continued to celebrate both the Sabbath and Sunday until around A.D. 360, when the Council of Laodicea forbade keeping both. Even before that, the focus had begun to shift from the Sabbath to Sunday. With Sunday accepted as the day for Christian worship, leaders still needed to decide on the form of worship and customs surrounding Sunday.

Form of Early Worship

An early non-Christian source gives us information about believers' services. Pliny the Younger (A.D. 113) served as governor of Bithynia under Emperor Trajan and sent a letter to the Emperor about the Christians in his province. He states "that they used to meet on a certain fixed day before dawn, and to recite in alternating verses a hymn to Christ as to a god."

Christians kept using the Roman term "sun day" because many of the early Church Fathers referred to Christ as the true Sun of Righteousness. This, added to the numerous references to Christ as light, made the sun a symbol of the Lord rising from His tomb.

Today's worship service looks much like that of the early believers. Justin, writing before A.D. 165, gives further insight into the form of worship.

"On the so-called "Day of the Sun" all of us, both from the city and from the farms, come together in one place, and the memories of the Apostles or the writings of the prophets are read, as time will permit."

After the reading, the day's leader spoke, urging the congregation to listen and apply what they had heard. They followed with prayer before bringing bread and wine. Before distributing the elements, the leader offered thanks for the bread and wine, and the people responded with "Amen." Deacons took portions to absent members after the services.

After the believers celebrated the Lord's Supper, they took an offering. The leader took charge of the money and distributed it to any in need. The church took particular care of orphans and widows, but any in need received a portion.

This form is similar to Jewish synagogue services. Reading from the Old Testament and then an explanation of the passage was a major part of Jewish worship. In the early church readings from the apostles or letters from church leaders added to the Old Testament readings.

Other traditions in our current worship spring from the earliest days of Christianity. In many churches, people stand for the Gospel reading. This goes back to early worship, when worshippers stood for the entire service. At this time, standing was an expression of respect and reverence. The idea has carried over into modern worship with people standing to show respect for the Gospel.

At the same time that standing was common in worship, kneeling was a position of servitude and slavery. Therefore, kneeling was not a common part of worship during the early days. Gradually people associated kneeling with penance or supplication and so began kneeling for prayer. Kneeling for communion became popular as the focus shifted to the divinity of Christ and the unworthiness of man.

Pews and sitting for services didn't come along until the sixteenth century. The Reformation spread the popularity of pews because services focused on teaching and preaching. As services grew longer, people needed to sit so they could concentrate on the message.

Sunday as a Day of Rest

The early church interpreted the commandment to "remember the Sabbath day by keeping it holy" to refer to any sinful activity on the Lord's Day. After Constantine, the idea of Sunday as a day of rest continued to grow. Some believers thought that if the Jews observed the Sabbath by not working, then Christians should observe Sunday even more strictly because the new covenant of Christ surpassed the old covenant of the law.

Later, as the church moved further from its Jewish roots and anti-Jewish sentiment arose, leaders condemned thinking of the Sabbath and Sunday as connected. Jerome and the later Council of Orleans in A.D. 538 rejected any connection between Judaism and Christianity, especially as concerned the laws of rest and the Christian Sunday.

The pendulum then swung back the other way. People began interpreting the Ten Commandments in a Christian context, and the church called for the discipline of any who worked on Sunday. The Council of Nabonne in A.D. 589 recommended severe punishment, including whipping, for those breaking Sunday rest. Then in A.D. 789 the Emperor Charlemagne ruled that any work on Sunday was a violation of the Ten Commandments, and the prohibition eventually passed into church law.

Today we still have a mixed group of ideas and laws regarding working on Sunday. In the early years of America, people wouldn't consider working on Sunday. Laws frequently upheld the common custom. Over the years, the laws have changed. Now many people go shopping on Sunday just as they would any other day of the week. Christians must decide individually how they will keep Sunday as a day of worship and rest, since the government no longer decides for us.

JANUARY

Let January's maiden be

all Garnet gemmed with constancy.*

Birthstone: Garnet

Birthstone Virtue: Constancy and faithfulness

Flower: Carnation

The Roman god, Janus, gave his name to January. Artists
showed Janus with two faces, and he was the god of beginnings
and endings, making him a logical choice for the first month of
the year.

*The couplets under each month comprise a larger traditional poem. See Willard A. Heaps,
Birthstones (New York: Meredith Press, 1969)

NEW YEAR'S CELEBRATIONS

January 1st

The eyes of the LORD your God are always upon it, from the beginning of the year to the end of the year.
Deuteronomy 11:12.

Because people associated the coming of a new year with change, throughout history they believed this was a perilous time when evil had more power. Our modern celebrations hold pieces of different rituals designed to help earlier people pass safely through this dangerous time.

The first part of early New Year's rituals was to deal with the end of the old year. Celebrants needed to throw out everything old to make way for the new. Fasts or other kinds of deprivation "used up" the last of the old year, and served as a form of cleansing to prepare for the New Year.

Perhaps the watch night services some churches hold do the same thing for us today. People held the first watch night service in 1770 at St. George's Methodist Church of Philadelphia, Pennsylvania. Such services help attendees begin the New Year in meditation, focusing on God.

The next step in older rituals was getting rid of evil, both personally and as a community. People removed personal evil by confessing sins, while taking care of the community by driving out demons. Many cultures utilized masked processions as part of New Year's celebrations. In this case, the masks usually represented the souls of the dead. Traditions might include a banquet or ceremony to welcome the dead. In the end, processions led the dead away from the living.

People also used noise to frighten evil away. Although firecrackers are the major modern day method of noise making, depending on where you live, you may also hear church bells, drums, car horns, sirens, boat whistles, or party horns. Today's noise is just for fun – not to frighten demons – but it goes back directly to ancient New Year's celebrations.

Once the old year had ended and people had removed evil from their area, they needed to start the New Year right. In some cultures they put out old fires before the end of the old year and then built new ones once the New Year began.

Some people staged fights between two opposing teams representing good and evil. In this case, they believed that good must win over evil to guarantee a good year. If you spend New Year's Day watching ball games on television, you could blame them on this old custom. Someone from an older culture would feel right at home watching the games.

Once the community had successfully started the New Year, they celebrated. Some chose feasts while others drank or engaged in other kinds of excesses. Today's drinking on New Year's has its roots in older celebrations of completing a difficult time. Excessive drinking may also be the remainder of an earlier custom that re-enacted on a personal level the chaos before God brought order into the cosmos.

A familiar symbol of New Year's, the Baby New Year made its first modern appearance in a fourteenth century German folk song. Even before then people called the New Year "the newborn one." The actual custom may have deeper roots, going back to ancient Greece and the festival of Dionysus. During this festival, celebrants paraded a baby cradled in a winnowing basket to symbolize the rebirth of Dionysus as the spirit of fertility.

EPIPHANY

January 6th

And going into the house they saw the child with Mary his mother, and they fell down and worshiped him. Then, opening their treasures, they offered him gifts, gold and frankincense and myrrh. Matthew 2:11.

What is the first holy day Christians celebrated? Not a Jewish holy day celebrated before Jesus' coming or even one celebrated in conjunction with His ministry. If you answered Christmas, or even Easter, you would be wrong, though believers celebrated the Resurrection before the Church established a fixed holy day.

Clement of Alexandria, Egypt, first mentioned Epiphany as a celebration at the end of the second century. As with other festivals, the date is close to non-Christian feasts from that time. January 6th was the Egyptians' winter solstice, at which they honored their sun god and Alexandrians celebrated the birth of their god, Acon, on January 5th.

We get the word epiphany from the Greek *epiphaneia*. Among the ancient Greeks, an epiphany was the appearance of a god or supernatural being or a festival commemorating such a visitation at a definite place. Christians celebrate three different events in Jesus' life at Epiphany. Each event revealed Christ to us in a different way.

First, the visit of the Magi to Jesus as a child showed Him as God of the Gentiles. Second, His baptism by John illustrated His divinity. Third, the miracle of water into wine at the wedding in Cana proved His divine power.

Eastern churches focus more on Jesus' baptism during Epiphany. In most Western churches – both Catholic and Protestant – you'll see the visit of the Magi emphasized. Since Epiphany follows closely after Christmas, this fits into the general holiday season.

The twelve days from Christmas to Epiphany form the liturgical celebration of Christmas. Many scholars believe the Magi visited after Jesus' birth, rather than being at the manger, making the interval between the celebration of Jesus' birth and the arrival of the Magi appropriate.

From the visit of the Magi, celebrated at Epiphany, come two other customs: the king cake and gift giving at Christmas. The king cake first appears as part of Epiphany at the end of the fourteenth century. Though people baked the cake in celebration of the Magi's visit, part of the celebration was to choose a "king" for the day. The cook added a coin, bean, or other object to the cake. The person who got the slice with the token became "king" of the celebration. This custom has now moved from Epiphany to modern Mardi Gras celebrations.

Originally, Christian leaders forbade giving gifts at Christmas because of the non-Christian association with the tradition. Romans of all ranks commonly exchanged gifts called *strenae* at New Year's celebrations that ran through the first days of the month. Since early Christians celebrated Christmas on January 6th, they strove to avoid any overlap from other celebrations around them.

So closely was the idea of gift giving tied to paganism that early Christians resisted the idea. Over time, though, Christian celebrations began including gift giving, with the explanation that their gifts commemorated the Magi's gifts to Jesus. Today we still hear the Magi as the reason for giving Christmas presents.

Over time, the proximity of early Christmas celebrations to Roman New Year's celebrations resulted in customs merging with Christmas celebrations, but not until few people still celebrated the old Roman observance and saw the old traditions as ways to add meaning to current practices.

FEBRUARY

In fitful February it's a verity

the amethyst denotes sincerity.

Birthstone: Amethyst

Birthstone Virtue: Prevention of violent passions

Flower: Violet

The Romans held special ceremonies of repentance on the 15th of this month. In Latin, *februare* means "to purify."

CANDLEMAS

February 2nd

*he took him up in his arms and blessed God and said, "Lord,
now you are letting your servant depart in peace,
according to your word; for my eyes have seen your
salvation that you have prepared in the presence of all
peoples, a light for revelation to the Gentiles, and for glory
to your people Israel." Luke 2:28-32.*

Candlemas commemorates Jesus' presentation at the temple and Mary's purification as required by Jewish law (see Lev. 12:6-8). After Jesus' birth, Mary and Joseph took Him to the temple to fulfill the Law. There the Holy Spirit directed Simeon to them. Luke's Gospel describes him as "righteous and devout," one who was waiting for the promised Messiah. Simeon took Jesus in his arms and praised God, declaring that he had now seen the long awaited Savior.

Simeon's declaration of Jesus' identity became the focus for Candlemas. About A.D. 390, a nun from northwestern Spain, Etheria, gave the first historical description. She kept a journal during her pilgrimage to Israel and gives us the first known information about many early church customs. Here, she tells of the celebration in Jerusalem beginning with a solemn procession in the morning, followed by a sermon on the gospel text, and ending with a mass.

During Etheria's time, people celebrated Candlemas on February fourteenth. The early Christians originally celebrated Jesus' birth at Epiphany on January sixth. Since Jesus' presentation was forty days after His birth, they simply called the day *Quadragesima de Epiphania* or "fortieth day after Epiphany." When leaders later agreed on December 25 for Christmas, the date for Candlemas moved to February second.

Some scholars believe that church leaders introduced Candlemas to counteract the Roman Lupercalia, because the early date of February fourteenth was close to Lupercalia on February fifteenth. A part of the celebration was a Feast of Purification connected with the goddess Ceres. According to myth, when Pluto, lord of the underworld, stole Ceres' daughter, Proserpine, Ceres looked for her by candlelight. People paraded through the city carrying candles or torches.

Other scholars claim no historical link exists between Candlemas and Lupercalia, since the Western church never held the festival of Mary's purification on February fourteenth. When a candlelight procession became a part of the Candlemas celebration in the seventh century, people hadn't celebrated Lupercalia for three hundred years.

The Eastern church celebrated Candlemas before Rome adopted it. In A.D. 542 Emperor Justinian ordered a celebration in Constantinople in thanksgiving for the end of plague in the city. From there, the celebration spread throughout the East.

Rome adopted Candlemas for the Western church during the seventh century. They gave it the name *Hypapante* or "the meeting," referring to Simeon meeting Jesus in the temple. At the same time, Pope Sergius I introduced the procession still a part of celebrations in the Catholic Church.

Churches that celebrate Candlemas still bless the candles used during the year. The candles point to Simeon's statement that Jesus was "a light for revelation to the Gentiles." This part of Candlemas began in the eighth century and became common by the eleventh century. England gives us the name Candlemas or "candle mass."

Despite the pre-Christian traditions, the Church intended candles used at Candlemas to have Christian symbolism. After the priest blesses and distributes them to the congregation, worshippers light them while they sing the *Nunc Dimittis* - Simeon's prayer. They carry the candles around the church, reminding us of the True Light of Christ entering into the world.

At one time, the Christmas season traditionally ended at Candlemas. People took down all decorations and stored them for the next year. They burned the Christmas greenery and spread the ashes over the fields to insure a good growing season.

GROUNDHOG DAY

February 2nd

While the earth remains, seedtime and harvest, cold and heat, summer and winter, day and night, shall not cease."
Genesis 8:22.

The idea that a groundhog and his shadow on February second tells us something about the weather seems to be a blend of two traditions brought to America. Part comes from a medieval belief that various hibernating animals come to the surface on Candlemas morning, also celebrated on February second, to observe the weather. In some places the hedgehog foretold the weather. In Germany, forecasts were the badger's responsibility. Immigrants to the U.S. transferred its abilities to the groundhog or woodchuck.

In England and Scotland, the weather on Candlemas determined future weather. If Candlemas was fair, then more winter was expected. If overcast, then winter was over. When people blended this idea with the groundhog, they believed that if the groundhog saw his shadow, there would be six more weeks of winter. If no shadow appeared, then winter was over.

Rhymes from England illustrate this tradition:

If Candlemas Day be dry and fair,
The half o' winter's to come and mair;
If Candlemas Day be wet and foul,
The half o' winters gone at Yule.

If Candlemas Day be fair and bright,
Winter will have another flight;
But if it be dark with clouds and rain,
winter is gone, and will not come again.

We don't know why the weather at Candlemas should have

anything to do with future weather.

The earliest known reference to Groundhog Day is an entry in storekeeper James L. Morris' diary dated February 4, 1841. As you can see, his entry verifies the German origin of the custom. He recalls:

"Last Tuesday, the 2nd was Candlemas day, the day on which, according to the Germans, the Groundhog peeps out of his winter quarters and if he sees his shadow he pops back for another six weeks nap, but if the day be cloudy he remains out, as the weather is to be moderate."

ST. VALENTINE'S DAY

February 14th

"This is my commandment, that you love one another as I have loved you. John 15:12.

Why a day dedicated to two or more Christian martyrs named Valentine came to be associated with lovers is a mystery, although we have several theories. Early lists of church martyrs show at least three men named Valentine. Some lists have as many as eight. For all, their feast day is February fourteenth.

The first three are the best known of the Valentines. We know the first from a list of martyred believers. Of the other two, one was a Roman priest and the other was the bishop of Interamna. Emperor Claudius II reportedly had both men beaten and beheaded in A.D. 269. What we know about these men gradually blended into a single figure.

You can find a number of legends around St. Valentine. One tells that while imprisoned, he cured the jailer's daughter of blindness. Another says that he fell in love with the jailer's daughter and sent her a letter signed "from your Valentine," thereby sending the very first Valentine greeting.

Another story relating to his eventual patronage of lovers takes place during the reign of Emperor Claudius II. The Emperor wanted to recruit men as soldiers, but they didn't want to leave their wives and sweethearts. Furious, the Emperor forbade marriages and canceled all engagements. Valentine, however, was sympathetic to young lovers and married several couples in secret. When the Emperor discovered what Valentine had done, he had him thrown in prison.

Another theory points to the Norman word *galatin*, meaning a lover of women. People once wrote and pronounced this word *valatan* or *valentin*. This idea makes sense, but we have no evidence for the idea.

Another more likely theory explains Valentine's Day as a Christianized form of the ancient Roman feast of Lupercalia. During the celebration, young men drew young women's names from a box. The young man who drew a woman's name became her partner for the festival.

Early Christian clergy objected to the pagan celebration and substituted the names of saints. During the following year the young man then attempted to emulate the saint he had drawn. People celebrated Lupercalia one day after Valentine's Day and the two merged over the years.

Still another possible explanation for the association of St. Valentine with lovers comes from the middle ages in Europe. People believed that birds began to mate on February fourteenth. Chaucer preserved evidence of this belief in his *Parliment of Foules*. He states, "For this was Seynt Valentyne's day. When every foul cometh ther to choose his mate."

We find later references to February fourteenth as Valentine's Day in Shakespeare, Drayton, and Pepys. In fact, Pepys shows us that gift giving and drawing for Valentines was common in his day. His diary entry for Valentine's Day 1667 reads in part,

"This morning came up to my wife's bedside (I being up dressing myself) little Will Mercer to be her valentine, and brought her name written upon blue paper in gold letters, done by himself, very pretty; and we were both well pleased with it."

Pepys goes on to tell that he was also his wife's Valentine, which cost him five pounds. He notes, though, that she would have cost him that, even if he hadn't been her Valentine. He records jewelry, some quite expensive, given as Valentine's gifts.

Credit for sending the first valentine goes to Charles, Duc D'Orleans. While imprisoned in the Tower of London after the Battle of Agincourt in 1415, he sent his wife valentine poems. Some point to this as the earliest evidence for the rhymed valentines popular throughout history. Others held that the Duke's letter was a one-time incident, not a tradition.

Researchers who discovered a 1477 Valentine's Day letter in England give us the oldest certain valentine. This letter's existence shows that people sent valentines not long after the poems sent by the Duc D'Orleans and would seem to uphold the idea that his letter represented a custom.

Margery Brews wrote the 1477 letter to her fiancé John Paston and addressed him as, "Right reverent and worshipful and my right well-beloved valentine." She also raised issues regarding her dowry, which Paston's father did not consider sufficient, and stated, "But if you love me, as I trust verily that you do, you will not leave me therefore." Apparently the letter worked, as the couple eventually married and had two sons.

By the seventeenth century, people began sending handmade valentines to their favorite. The style depended entirely on the maker. The first commercial valentines came out around 1800. Cards varied from elaborate, with lace and flowers, to the "penny dreadfuls" or inexpensive put down cards. People called them "penny dreadfuls" because they cost only a penny and the designs were dreadful.

In the United States, exchanging valentine cards probably reached an all-time high during the Civil War. An 1863 periodical published in Boston said of Valentine's Day that "with the exception of Christmas there is no festival throughout the year which is invested with half the interest belonging to this cherished anniversary."

In the first third of the twentieth century, children began observing the custom of sending valentines. The valentine "mail box" where children could "mail" cards for their classmates became a common feature.

Now you can buy valentines for everyone, from friends and family on through business associates and casual acquaintances. From being a festival mainly for lovers, Valentine's Day has become a time to express appreciation and friendship on all levels.

Valentine's Day Symbols

Cupid

One of the most enduring symbols of Valentine's Day is Cupid. In Roman mythology he is the god of love, taken from his Greek counterpart, Eros. According to most myths, Cupid was the son of Venus, Aphrodite in Greek, goddess of love and beauty. In earlier stories writers described him simply as a slender youth.

The later, better known stories, showed Cupid as a naked, winged boy carrying a bow and arrows. Cupid was often mischievous and frequently caused problems with his arrows. When he shot either humans or gods in the heart with the arrows, they fell in love.

During Hellenistic times, artists multiplied Eros (Cupid) from one god into many "cupids" on frescos or ceramics. We now see the cupid Christianized as a baby angel.

Heart

In many early traditions, people considered the heart the seat of emotions and affections, functions we now believe belong to the brain. During the Middle Ages, people romanticized the heart and the stylized heart shape was born.

No one seems to be certain why the current shape came to stand for a heart, though people raised various possibilities. One source suggests that the heart is a stylized human buttock, or perhaps suggests a female torso. Others theorize the heart comes from the imprint of a kiss on paper. Regardless, we now see the heart as a universal symbol of love and affection.

PURIM

Date varies - February/March

And who knows whether you have not come to the kingdom for such a time as this?" Esther 4:14.

Purim celebrates Esther and Mordecai's victory over Haman as told in the book of Esther. The modern Jewish observance includes reading the book of Esther, along with a festive family meal, sending gifts of food to friends, giving money for the poor, costumes, masquerades, plays, and heavy drinking.

The book of Esther tells of a young Jewish girl named Hadassah. The Persian king, Xerxes, took her into his harem after banishing the previous queen, Vashti. Hadassah was renamed Esther and became the new queen.

Meanwhile, outside the palace, her cousin, Mordecai, became embroiled in a power struggle with Haman, the king's Grand Vizier. When Mordecai refused to bow to Haman as the king had ordered, Haman created a plan to exterminate all Jews in the Persian Empire. Mordecai sent word to Esther, who had kept her Jewish identity secret. She agreed to go to King Xerxes, even though he had not summoned her, an act that could result in death.

King Xerxes extended his scepter, granting her life, when she appeared before him. This gave Esther the opportunity to match wits with Haman. In the end Haman was discredited and executed. Mordecai received Haman's former position, and helped save the Jewish people from extermination.

Scholars attack Esther more than any other book in the Bible.

Only Esther never mentions God, and some scholars argue that the book is not historical. Others point out the importance of fasting in Esther, which Jewish people always accompanied with prayer. The text implies God's presence without mentioning it directly. Both Jewish leaders and Christian leaders accepted the book as part of their Holy Scriptures, and modern Jews still celebrate Esther's courage.

Participants in modern Purim celebrations often bring noisemakers or stomp and hiss each time the reader speaks Haman's name. Others write Haman's name on the soles of their shoes and stamp until erasing the name.

Holding satiric plays and skits poking fun at rabbis or members of the synagogue usually held in reverence is another tradition. Celebrations in Israel include the injunction to drink until you can't tell the difference between cursed Haman and blessed Mordecai.

MARCH

But oh, what shall a March maid do?

Wear a bloodstone and be firm and true.

Birthstone: Bloodstone, Aquamarine

Birthstone Virtue: Steadfast affection, courage, and wisdom

Flower: Jonquil

Mars, the Roman god of war, gave his name to March.

ST. PATRICK'S DAY

March 17th

And he said to them, "Go into all the world and proclaim the gospel to the whole creation. Mark 16:15.

Perhaps you shared a common problem on St. Patrick's Day during your school years. Even if you weren't Catholic, you'd still probably heard about St. Patrick and knew that you were supposed to wear green. If you forgot, you joined the other unfortunates in dodging pinches all day long or maybe arguing for the small bit of green in the pattern of your shirt.

Despite being one of the best known saints, we know very little for certain about St. Patrick. Though considered the patron saint of Ireland, he was not born there. In fact, we don't know his exact birthplace. In his book Confession, he gives his birthplace as *Bannauem Taberniae*, though no one now knows where the village was located. People have suggested various possible locations for his birth including Kilpatrick near Dumbarton, Scotland; near Glastonbury, England; Monmouthshire, England; Tours, France; or Wales.

Nor do we know if the date of his celebration, March 17, is his birth date or death date. Different sources make different claims. It may be neither. Various sources also give a range of possible dates for his birth year. Possibilities range from A.D. 373, 386, 387, 389, to 395. He died either in 461 or around 492. Some legends say that he died at 120 years of age as Moses did.

To add to the confusion, some scholars believe that there were two men named Patrick. Over the years people combined the stories about them into one man. Stories of miracles he performed during his lifetime muddle the situation further. In his own writings he never claimed to have performed a miracle, though he may have done so.

Patrick's original name was Maewyn. His family's English name was Succat, meaning clever in war. He frequently spoke of himself in his writings as *patricius* or well born, giving us the English Patrick. Speaking of himself as "well born" does seem to go against his well-known humility. In fact, the Irish people nicknamed him and familiarly called him "Old Shaved Head."

Patrick's own words are the best place for factual information. He opens his book, *Confessions*, with a brief history of his life.

"I, Patrick, a sinner, the most rustic and the least of all the faithful, and in the estimation of very many deemed contemptible, had for my father Calpornius, a deacon, the son of Potitus, a presbyter, who belonged to the village of Bannauem Taberniae; for close thereto he had a small villa, where I was made a captive.

At the time I was barely 16 years of age, I knew not the true God; and I was led to Ireland in captivity with many thousand persons according to our deserts, for we turned away from God and kept not His commandments, and we were not obedient to our priests who used to admonish us about our salvation. And the Lord brought us the indignation of His wrath, and scattered us amongst many nations even to the utmost part of the earth, where now my littleness may be seen amongst strangers.

And there the Lord opened the understanding of my unbelief so that at length I might recall to mind my sins and be converted with all my heart to the Lord, my God, who hath regarded my humility and taken pity on my youth and my ignorance, and kept watch over me before I knew Him, and before I had discretion, and could distinguish between good and evil; and He protected me and consoled me as a father does his son."

"I was made a captive" refers to his capture at age sixteen by brigands, who took him to Ireland. They sold him into slavery to a chieftain named Miliuc, for whom Patrick worked as a shepherd. During this time he became a Christian.

After six years as a slave, he had a vision in which he saw a ship provided to return him to his family. He followed the vision and escaped on a boat carrying a cargo of Irish hounds to the Continent. From there he returned home to his parents.

His return home was short lived. Soon after returning, he had another vision. He saw a man bearing a letter that asked him to return to the people of Ireland, which he believed was a call from God. This time he went as a missionary to share the good news of Christ with the Irish people.

He began preparing for his mission by going back to Europe from Britain. There he studied under the bishop of Auxerre, Germanus. At first, his superiors in the church would not allow him to go to Ireland. Leaders turned down Patrick to become the bishop of Ireland. In his place, they sent a man named Palladius.

Palladius' time in Ireland was short. He died the following spring. In 432 Pope Celestine I ordained Patrick as bishop and allowed him to return. Some time in the spring or summer of that year, he and his companions set foot on Irish soil.

The native Druid priests opposed his ministry. Patrick ignored their protests and continued with his work. Among other things, he began a tradition that continues to this day of lighting an Easter fire. At the time, he did so to counter the Druids' spring fire. He also caused consternation when he christened the Druids' fires, making them a symbol of Christ, the Light of the World.

By the end of his life, most people in Ireland had converted to Christianity. His followers finished the job within a few years after his death.

One of the more common stories about St. Patrick – how he used a shamrock to explain the Trinity – may be authentic. He mentioned the Trinity often in his writings. Tradition claims he wrote two hymns, "St. Patrick's Breastplate" and "The Deer's Cry," which both speak of the Trinity. In "St. Patrick's Breastplate" he sings of "Three in One, and One in Three." In "The Deer's Cry," the mention is clearer:

"I arise today
Through a mighty strength, the invocation of the Trinity,
Through belief in the threeness,
Through confession of the oneness
Of the Creator of Creation."

He explained the shamrock's three leaves represented the Father, the Son, and the Holy Spirit. A single stem, representing the Godhead, joined them. Just as the Father, the Son, and the Holy Spirit are all separate and yet are One God, the leaves of the shamrock are separate yet make up one plant.

In doing so, he chose to take a pagan symbol and gave it Christian meaning. He may have chosen to emphasize the Trinity because three was the number of the Druids' unknown god. They originally used the shamrock in Celtic fertility rites. They burned the plants and spread the ashes on the fields to promote the crops' growth. Regardless of the early associations with fertility rites, the shamrock was an excellent way to make a difficult idea approachable to the people.

Another familiar story about Patrick is that he drove all the snakes out of Ireland. Some look at this as a literal removal of snakes. Others believe that this was a symbolic statement referring to the Druids. A snake often stood for their wisdom. St. Patrick drove the serpent of Druidic wisdom away, replacing it with the truth of Christ.

St. Patrick's Day in America goes back before the Revolution. The Charitable Irish Society of Boston held the first celebration in 1737. People founded the Society "for the relief of the poor and indigent Irishmen reduced by sickness, shipwreck, old age or other infirmities." Oddly, given the association of St. Patrick and the Irish with Catholicism, the organization was Protestant.

St. Patrick also took part in American history. During the British evacuation of Boston on March 17, 1776, the colonial forces at Cambridge used "Boston" as the password and "St. Patrick" as the countersign. Even if celebrations weren't yet common, people knew about St. Patrick.

The Friendly Sons of St. Patrick celebrated March 17th in Philadelphia in 1780. Irish veterans of the Revolutionary War organized the New York branch of the society in 1784. The organization included both Protestants and Catholics. In fact, the first president was a Presbyterian.

Today you may automatically think of the "wearin' of the green" with St. Patrick's Day, but this custom didn't begin until over one thousand years after St. Patrick's death. Originally, people associated the blue with Saint Patrick. Over the years the color green became associated with Saint Patrick's Day instead, perhaps because of the green in the Irish flag and Ireland's identification as "the Emerald Isle." People wore green ribbons and shamrocks to celebrate as early as the seventeenth century.

That pinching problem came even later as an American tradition. Around the early 1700s celebrants thought wearing green made you invisible to leprechauns, who would pinch anyone they could see. After the custom came to America, people began doing the pinching themselves for those who didn't wear green as a reminder that the leprechauns could see them.

MARDI GRAS

Date varies – March

*I acknowledged my sin to you, and I did not cover my iniquity;
I said, "I will confess my transgressions to the LORD," and
you forgave the iniquity of my sin. Psalm 32:5.*

The words *mardi gras* literally mean *fat Tuesday* (French). Strictly speaking, Mardi Gras is the Tuesday before the beginning of Lent, which starts on Ash Wednesday. You can trace the name to the tradition of using up all eggs, milk, and fat in preparation for the forty days of Lent. During the Lenten fast, the church prohibited eating all of those products. In the days before refrigeration, they would spoil before the fast was over. Since pancakes became a traditional way to use up these materials, people also called Mardi Gras "pancake day."

People in England called it Shrove Tuesday from the practice of confessing sins in preparation for Lent. "To shrive" means to confess and receive absolution.

The other side of Mardi Gras is carnival, the best known being the yearly celebration in New Orleans. Many believe this aspect comes from pre-Christian fertility and spring rites, and various new year's customs. Early Egyptians, as well as Greeks and Romans celebrated during this time of year.

Another source points out that five centuries separate the last mention of pagan rites similar to carnival and the first medieval mention of the word. Writers last mentioned Lupercalia in A.D. 494. We don't see *Carnelevare* first mentioned until A.D. 965. The source suggests that carnival developed along with the church's rules about

Lent. He further suggests that the church may have fostered the pagan association to help suppress the festival's disorderliness.

The word *carnival* comes from the Latin *carne vale* or "farewell meat." In this case, the meat refers to Lenten fasting, which begins the next day. At one time, carnival extended from Epiphany to Shrove Tuesday, though this is not usually the case today.

During the Middle Ages, Florence and Venice were famous for their carnival pageantry, including floats, costumes, and masks. In Venice, flower clad gondolas added to the celebration. Celebrations in Rome included participants throwing confetti at each other. Spanish cities staged carnivals and balls, while the Portuguese held floral balls and mock battles with confetti. The French held costume balls along with float filled parades and flower battles.

During the colonial era in America, French settlers along coastal areas from present day New Orleans, LA to Mobile, AL celebrated carnival sporadically. Various documents point to celebrations, but don't show an unbroken line of celebration from settlement to the present. Both New Orleans and Mobile held – and hold – the largest carnival celebrations in America.

Some sources say that modern Mardi Gras came to America from France in 1827, when a group of students who had been studying in France came back to New Orleans and brought the custom with them. Another extensive source referred to this as a tall tale from various tourist brochures. He offers enough evidence of regular celebrations before this date to uphold the idea that we can't trace Mardi Gras to a single point in time.

The modern form of Mardi Gras began in Mobile with the introduction of the first krewe, the Cowbellion de Rakin Society. The society formed on New Year's Eve and probably drew from the German *belsnickle* tradition on Christmas Eve. Before long the Society began parading at Mardis Gras and both the Society and tradition moved to New Orleans where it continued to develop.

The traditional colors for Mardi Gras are gold, green, and purple, dating back to 1872 when the organization Rex designed a royal flag for the "king" of Mardi Gras. The now traditional flag has a diagonal bar of gold from the upper left corner to the lower right corner, with an upper triangle of green and a purple lower triangle. A crown rests in the center of the gold bar.

One source interprets the colors as purple standing for royalty, gold for purity, and green for love and friendship. However, in the Rex parade of 1892, with the theme "Symbolism of Colors," the organization identified purple with justice, green with faith, and gold with power. Regardless, the colors provide a rich background for the celebrations.

The carnival aspects of Mardi Gras have nearly taken over the Christian ones. What was originally a day of preparation for Lent has now become an all-out extravaganza.

ASH WEDNESDAY

Date varies – March

therefore I despise myself, and repent in dust and ashes." Job 42:6.

After Mardi Gras – the day, not the carnival season – comes Ash Wednesday and the beginning of Lent. Participants attending Ash Wednesday services receive the sign of the cross marked in blessed ashes on their foreheads. Frequently, the church saves palms from the previous year's Palm Sunday celebration and burns them for Ash Wednesday services.

Originally, only "public sinners," received the ashes: those who had committed a serious public sin and were undergoing penance to be received back into the church. Usually repentance was a private matter, but serious sin called for public repentance. Penance wasn't easy. The term lasted from Ash Wednesday to Holy Thursday and involved many restrictions.

Frequently, penitents were required to live in a monastery apart from others, performing manual labor. In addition, they might be required to abstain from meat, alcohol, bathing, haircuts, shaves, marriage relations, and business transactions. From this forty-day period of separation comes our word *quarantine*.

Though first intended only for public sinners, gradually other devout Christians began volunteering to receive ashes on this day. By the end of the eleventh century, the custom had become widespread rather than being restricted to notorious sinners.

Actually, Ash Wednesday is forty-six days before Easter, but forty days before Holy Week, which begins with Palm Sunday. People called Ash Wednesday "Beginning of the Fast" until 1099 when Pope Urban II gave it the current name.

Some have found the change from the party atmosphere to Ash Wednesday's repentance hard to understand. In 1592, Ogier Ghislain de Busbecq, an ambassador from Emperor Ferdinand I to the court of Sultan Suleiman I, wrote a letter which told of a Turkish official who went to Europe on a diplomatic mission for the sultan and witnessed the carnival festivities prior to Lent. When he returned to Constantinople, he reported his observations to the sultan. According to his account, Christians went completely mad during a certain time of year, but when their priests sprinkled ashes on them, they immediately became sane. While this may be a tall tale, Pope Benedict XIV took it seriously and quoted the account in his letter protesting the abuses of carnival celebrations.

In liturgical churches, the arrival of Lent includes removing the alleluia sung during services. Alleluia comes from Hebrew for "Praise the Lord." Church leaders considered it out of keeping with the sorrowful nature of Lent. In the early church, people only used alleluia at Easter, but later it spread to the rest of the year except for Lent. The alleluia returns to the church during the Mass of the Easter Vigil on the Saturday before Easter, foreshadowing the Resurrection.

LENT

Date varies- March/April

"Yet even now," declares the LORD, "return to me with all your heart, with fasting, with weeping, and with mourning;
Joel 2:12.

Our word Lent comes from the Anglo-Saxon *lencten*, meaning spring. Christians in Egypt established the traditional forty days of Lent before A.D. 330. Today people think of the forty days of Lent as remembering Jesus' forty days in the wilderness before He began His ministry. Forty shows up several places in Scripture. Moses spent forty days in the wilderness, the Jews wandered forty years before God allowed them to enter the Promised Land, and Jonah gave Nineveh forty days to repent.

In the early church, new converts fasted for forty hours to prepare for baptism on Easter Eve. The Latin name, *Quadragesima*, reflects that tradition. Later, the emphasis switched from preparing new believers for baptism to penitence for all believers.

When Emperor Constantine made Christianity the official state religion of the Roman Empire in the fourth century, church leaders worried that the sudden increase in members would change the church's character. They tried to prevent this by requiring all Christians to participate in the Lenten fast.

Today most people think of fasting at Lent in terms of what they will give up. Fasting in the early days was a much more severe discipline. Pope Gregory defined fasting for the church at large in a letter to Saint Augustine in A.D. 604. "We abstain from flesh meat and from all things that come from flesh, as milk, cheese, eggs." The church considers Sundays a "little Easter" each week and exempts Sundays from fasting.

At least one Lenten food has been around since the Roman Empire. Christians used special dough consisting only of flour, salt, and water, conforming to the strictest possible fasting guidelines. They then shaped the dough like two arms crossed in prayer to remind them that Lent was a season of penance.

They called the bread *bracellae* or "little arms" in Latin. In German it became *brezel* or *prezel*. In English, of course, we know them as pretzels. The oldest known picture of a pretzel is in a fifth century Vatican manuscript. Eating pretzels year round became common during the nineteenth century, and their previous Lenten meaning was lost.

Another story of the pretzel comes much later. In this version, an Italian monk in A.D. 610 created pretzels when he used leftover bread dough to bake gifts for children who learned their prayers. He called them *pretiola* or "little reward." In this version, the twist still represents arms crossed in prayer, with the three holes representing the Trinity.

Perhaps both are correct. The monk could easily have used the more austere Lenten pretzels as an idea and substituted bits of bread dough. Regardless of which story is correct, the pretzel originated within the church.

Draping the Cross

Many churches today drape an outdoor cross with fabric in liturgical colors to share the Easter season with the community. Inside, of course, the paraments on the altar and the clergy's vestments change color, too. Purple is the liturgical color of Lent and symbolizes penitence, so the first cloth is purple.

The purple cloth remains in place until Good Friday, when people replace the purple with black, as a symbol of mourning for Jesus' crucifixion and death. The black cloth stays up until Easter Sunday, when a white cloth replaces the black one. White symbolizes the great joy of the Resurrection.

A related custom shares the meaning of Easter with passersby. It begins like the draped cross, with a plain wooden cross in front of the church at the beginning of Lent. Some churches include a crown of thorns. On Easter Sunday morning, congregation members bring flowers from their homes to decorate the plain wood. The unadorned cross becomes a floral reminder of the new life Jesus' resurrection gives.

PALM SUNDAY

Date varies - March/April

So they took branches of palm trees and went out to meet him, crying out, "Hosanna! Blessed is he who comes in the name of the Lord, even the King of Israel!" John 12:13.

With Palm Sunday, Lent ends and Holy Week begins. Throughout the week leading up to Easter Sunday, we remember and celebrate the events of Jesus' last week before the crucifixion. On the first Palm Sunday, Jesus rode into Jerusalem on a donkey and the people greeted him with palm branches. At that time, a king rode to war on a horse. A king who came in peace, however, rode on a donkey.

Jesus proclaimed Himself to be the King of the Jews by choosing to ride a donkey into Jerusalem. Many recognized Him as the long awaited Messiah, but some missed the symbolism of the donkey. They were still waiting for a warrior king to lead them against the Romans. Jesus came in peace to offer personal – not political – redemption.

We find the first reference to a Palm Sunday procession Etheria's travel journal. She mentions seeing a procession on her pilgrimage to Jerusalem and describes it.

. . .all the children in the neighborhood, even those who are too young to walk, are carried by their parents on their shoulders, all of them bearing branches, some of palms and some of olives, and thus the bishop is escorted in the same manner as the Lord was of old. For all, even those of rank, both matrons and men, accompany the bishop all

40

the way on foot in this manner, making these responses, from the top of the mount to the city, and thence through the whole city to the Anastasis, going very slowly lest the people should be wearied. . .

Cyril, Bishop of Jerusalem, instituted the Palm Sunday ritual between A.D. 382 and 386. For the Western church, the first reported observance is in Spain, probably in the fifth century. Oddly, Roman Christians did not celebrate the day before the twelfth century.

APRIL

The April girl has a brave defense.

The diamond guards her innocence.

Birthstone: Diamond

Birthstone Virtue: Purity, repentance, and innocence

Flower: Sweetpea

The month's name is uncertain. It may come from a form of Aphrodite, *Aprilis*, the goddess of love.

APRIL FOOL'S DAY

April 1st

The way of a fool is right in his own eyes, but a wise man listens to advice. Proverbs 12:15.

Like all children, you probably relished April Fool's Day. Tricking adults with far-fetched stories delights the child in all of us. In fact, a festival in India bears a striking resemblance to April Fool's Day, though most scholars feel that the similarity is a coincidence.

One favorite form of April fooling is sending someone on a fool's errand, such as asking for a biography of Adam's grandfather. We can see how old this tradition is from this 1760 verse in Poor Robin's Almanac.

"The first of April, some do say,
Is set apart for All Fools' Day.
But why the people call it so,
Nor I, nor they themselves do know.
But on this day are people sent
On purpose for pure merriment."

One story suggested for the beginning of April Fool's Day involves a fool's errand. According to Roman mythology, the god of the underworld, Pluto, kidnapped Proserpine, the daughter of the goddess Ceres. Ceres heard her daughter's cries for help and began searching for her, as any mother would do. People considered it a fool's errand because no one but Pluto could enter the underworld and return.

Another legend offered as explanation was "The Wise Men of Gotham," a story from the reign of King John in the 1200s. He wanted to walk through the meadow in Gotham, but, according to the custom of the day, anywhere the king walked became a public road. The people of Gotham didn't want their meadow to become a public roadway, so they prevented the king from walking there.

Angry, the king sent back an officer to find out why the people had refused him and to punish them. The people heard about the officer coming and had only a short time to think of a plan to defuse the king's anger. When the king's officer arrived he discovered the townspeople doing a variety of foolish things. Some tried to drown fish in a pond. Others dragged wagons onto barn roofs to shade the roof from the sun. Still others rolled cheeses down the hill, saying that they would find their own way to the Nottingham market.

As a result, the official returned to the king and told him that they were all fools. The king didn't need to bother with punishing them. In this way, they fooled the king and escaped punishment.

The most likely source for April Fool's Day is the calendar changeover in France. Before the change, people commonly celebrated the New Year throughout the week following March twenty-fifth. Most French people exchanged visits and gave gifts on April 1, the last day of the New Year's seven day celebration or octave.

When Charles IX proclaimed January 1 as New Year's Day in 1564, people needed several years to recognize the change. Part of the problem was poor communication, but more conservative members of society resisted the change. Those who had embraced the new custom ridiculed the conservatives by making mock solemn visits on April 1 and sending gag gifts.

In England and the British colonies, the change to the new calendar came later, between 1751 and1752. People may have carried the custom of April fooling into England from France at that point in time.

Though this idea makes sense, people in America knew about April Fool's Day before the calendar changeover took place. Puritan Judge Sewall notes in his diary,

"In the morning I dehorted Sam Hirst and Grindell Rawson from playing idle tricks because 'twas the first of April: They were the greatest fools that did so. N.E. men came hither to avoid anniversary days, the keeping of them such as 25th Decr. How displeasing must it be to God the giver of our Time to keep anniversary days to play the fool with ourselves and others."

Since Sewall lived from March 28, 1652 to January 1, 1730 he wrote well before the calendar changeover. The English settlers had apparently brought the custom of April Fool's Day to the New World with them.

MAUNDY THURSDAY

Date varies - March/April

Then he poured water into a basin and began to wash the disciples' feet and to wipe them with the towel that was wrapped around him. John 13:5.

Maundy Thursday commemorates the Last Supper, Jesus' agony in the Garden, and His arrest. Etheria, who gave us the first account of a Palm Sunday procession, also gives an account of pilgrims receiving the Eucharist in commemoration of the first Eucharist. People had not started using the name Maundy Thursday, but the description is similar to services held today.

During the ceremony, the pilgrims stopped in Gethsemane at the traditional spot where Judas betrayed Jesus. Leaders read the report of Jesus' arrest, resulting in "so great a moaning and groaning of all the people, together with weeping, that their lamentation may be heard perhaps as far as the city."

The term *maundy* comes from the Latin *mandatum* (commandment), another tie to the Last Supper. Jesus' statement at the Last Supper in Latin is *Mandatum novum do vobis*: "A new commandment I give you" John 13:34.

Church services today vary. Most will include the Lord's Supper. Some churches have a tenebrae service. People leave in darkness and silence to contemplate Jesus' sacrifice. Extinguishing the lights shows the temporary victory of darkness over light.

Other churches include foot washing, remembering Jesus washing the disciples' feet before the Last Supper. In Rome, the Pope washes the feet of thirteen officials. The first twelve represent the apostles. The final person stands for the angel who appeared at the table when Gregory the Great carried out the custom in the sixth century.

GOOD FRIDAY

Date varies - March/April

And when they came to the place that is called The Skull, there they crucified him, and the criminals, one on his right and one on his left. Luke 23:33.

Why we call the day of Jesus' crucifixion good is a mystery. Some sources suggest that *good* is a corruption of God's Friday. Others say that good refers to the good gift of salvation given on the cross. Other names for the day include Festival of the Crucifixion, Day of Salvation, Long Friday, and Holy Friday. We know that the Good Friday practice of the Veneration of the Cross, a custom still observed in Catholic churches, goes back to Etheria's day.

Eating hot cross buns is one of the oldest customs associated with Good Friday. This custom may have a pre-Christian origin. The Egyptians used small loaves stamped with symbolic horns in their worship of Isis. Greeks used cross-marked cakes associated with the goddess Diana. Archeologists discovered two small loaves with crosses on them in the ash covered ruins of Herculaneum, buried since the eruption of Mt. Vesuvius in A.D. 79.

Early Christians celebrated with flat unleavened cakes similar to Passover loaves. Later people made the cakes with the same dough used to make the bread for communion. Hot cross buns are most popular in England, where tradition says they originated in 1361, when a monk at St. Alban's Abbey baked them to give to the poor. Just as with other customs, an older pagan tradition existed, but the modern one began many years after from the earlier one.

EASTER

Date varies - March/April

*Blessed be the God and Father of our Lord Jesus Christ!
According to his great mercy, he has caused us to be born
again to a living hope through the resurrection of Jesus Christ
from the dead, I Peter 1:3.*

The early Christians began remembering the Resurrection every Sunday following its occurrence. In A.D. 325, the Council of Nicaea in 325 set aside a special day just to celebrate the Resurrection. The problem with an official day was deciding whether believers should celebrate the Resurrection on a weekday – figured from the Jewish Passover as the original Resurrection happened – or always on a Sunday.

Many felt that Passover should determine the date to celebrate the Resurrection. Once Jewish leaders determined the date of Passover, Christian leaders would set Easter three days later. Following this schedule meant that Easter would be a different day of the week each year, only occasionally falling on a Sunday.

Others believed that since the Lord rose on a Sunday, and this day had been set aside as the Lord's Day, only Sunday would do to celebrate His resurrection. As Christianity drew away from Judaism, some were reluctant to base the Christian celebration on the Jewish calendar.

Finally the Council decided Christians should celebrate Easter on the Sunday following the first full moon after the vernal equinox. Since the date of the vernal equinox changed from year to year, calculating the proper date could be difficult. This is still the method used to determine Easter today, which is why some years we have Easter earlier than other years.

Since Easter is a celebration of Jesus' Resurrection, you would think there wouldn't be room for paganism. However, Easter symbols intertwine pagan symbolism and ritual with church customs.

We aren't certain where we get the word *easter*. The Venerable Bede, an eighth century monk and scholar, suggested the word may have come from the Anglo-Saxon *Eostre* or *Eastre* - a Teutonic goddess of spring and fertility whose symbol was the hare. Recent scholars have not been able to find any reference to the goddess Bede mentioned and consider the theory discredited.

Another possibility is the Norse *eostur, eastur,* or *ostara* which meant "the season of the growing sun" or "the season of new birth." The word east comes from the same roots. In this case, *easter* would be linked to the changing of the season rather than a pagan goddess. Perhaps Bede confused the season, marked by a variety of celebrations, with a goddess.

A more recent and complex explanation comes from the Christian background of Easter rather than the pagan. The early Latin name for the week of Easter was *hebdomada alba* or "white week," while the Sunday after Easter day was called *dominica in albis* from the white robes of those who had been newly baptized. The word *alba* is Latin both for white and dawn. People speaking Old High German made a mistake in their translation and used a plural word for dawn, *ostarun*. From *ostarun* we get the German *Ostern* and the English Easter.

Some sources state that Easter comes from the Babylonian goddess Ishtar. The earlier Akkadian spelling of the name, Estar, comes even closer, but the resemblance is coincidental. According to Dr. Joe E. Lunceford, "Etymologically there is probably no connection between Ishtar and Easter." He points to the Greek word for east as the origin.

The Ishtar Question

When you begin writing about the origins of holidays, especially from a Christian perspective, problems come up almost immediately. People have different interpretations of Scripture and different denominational backgrounds. Some have more sensitive consciences, as Paul points out in I Corinthians 8-10 in his discussion of pagan customs. For them, a holiday with any connection to paganism may be a problem. Others have no issue with the past. Then when you add children to the mix, with their limited understanding, the questions can become more complex.

Sometimes research can't find all the answers. One source may choose the most likely option and present it as the only one. Other sources will list a variety. Newer sources may discredit older ones with fresh research.

The connection between Ishtar and Easter is one of the most challenging questions to answer because sources present two different sets of information. Google "Ishtar" and "Easter" together and you get a list of websites that explain Easter comes from the Babylonian goddess Ishtar. Further, the goddess's symbol was an egg, and she made rabbits lay eggs by touching them. According to many, these symbols of a pagan religion have infiltrated the Christian faith.

Google "Ishtar" alone and a different set of websites come up. They agree that Ishtar was a Mesopotamian goddess – the area including Babylon. People also knew her as Inana in Sumerian. Ishtar's worship influenced that of the Canaanite goddess Astarte or Ashtoreth and the Greek goddess Aphrodite. But you don't find any mention of eggs or rabbits.

To try to understand these two sets of information, we have to follow two different paths. The first path leads to Ishtar and the Babylonian religion by way of the Protestant Reformation. To begin we go to the Old Testament and the Babylonian captivity of the Israelites.

Scripture tells us that King Nebuchadnezzar took many Israelites to Babylon after he captured Jerusalem in 586 B.C. The Babylonian captivity made a deep impression on the Jewish people and reminded them of the price they paid if they disobeyed God. Their captivity lasted seventy years, until the later King Cyrus allowed them to return to Israel.

Much later, Catholics borrowed the term "Babylonian Captivity" when the papacy moved from Rome to Avignon in France. Opponents of the move called this "The Babylonian Captivity of the Papacy." Later the papacy returned to Rome, but this period gives us a connection between the church and Babylon.

Martin Luther used the title and idea in a treatise titled *On the Babylonian Captivity of the Church*, in which he states that "I now know of a certainty that the papacy is the kingdom of Babylon and the power of Nimrod the mighty hunter." The remainder of the material addresses the seven sacraments and seems to use the Babylonian captivity as a symbol, not a literal acceptance of Babylonian religion. As the Israelites were captives in Babylon, so were the Christians of his day captives of the church.

Luther was one of many calling for reform in the Catholic Church. Others called for more radical reform and began attacking Catholicism as a whole. (See the earlier section on church history.) These reformers wanted to remove anything not mentioned in Scripture, which included holy days and various customs. People died as martyrs on both sides of the question. As this pressure increased, so did the voices of the reformers against Catholicism.

After Reform penetrated Scotland and the Church of Scotland became the predominant religious institution, tensions remained high. Part of the problem was political, not just religious. The British monarchy moved back and forth from Catholic to Protestant, leaving the other side facing persecution each time.

Sir George Sinclair, the second Baronet of Ulbster, wrote prolifically against Catholicism, including a compilation of *Letters to the Protestants of Scotland*. These letters from the mid-1800s focus on the errors of Catholicism, but also speak of Catholicism as Christianized paganism, picking up the earlier theme of Babylonian religion.

This theme inspired another writer who seems to be at the root of the modern link between Easter and Ishtar. Rev. Alexander Hislop's *The Two Babylons or the Papal Worship Proved to Be the Worship of Nimrod and his Wife* directly acknowledges Sir George Sinclair as inspiring his work. Unlike the earlier writers who used Babylon as a metaphor, Rev. Hislop attempted to prove that Catholicism was a direct descendant of early Babylonian religion. The book, now in its fourth edition, still influences many people today.

In *The Two Babylons* Rev. Hislop takes similarities between any god or goddess as proof that they all are the same as Nimrod or Semiramis (Nimrod's wife), who eventually works down to being the same as Ishtar and the other goddesses in his estimation. Once every religious system outside of Christianity becomes worship of Nimrod or Semiramis, any symbols belonging to any god or goddess belong to all.

Hislop also addresses festivals, including both Easter and Christmas. Here we find the connection of Ishtar/Astarte to Easter. He gives as evidence his assumptions of connection between Druid worship in Britain and Baal worship.

Other authors have accepted Hislop's conclusions and written further about the various connections. Here the first path ends with many people convinced that the Catholic Church and Babylonian religion are the same. Further, customs that came through Catholicism are pagan and Christians should reject them.

This takes us to the second path, which begins with Babylonian religion and attempts to trace the connections Hislop puts forth in historical documents. Syncretism does occur within religions. Older traditions often merged with newer ones when cultures met. Gods or goddesses who performed the same function merged into one within the dominant culture. A quick survey of Mesopotamian religions provides clear evidence that Ishtar's worship did influence other goddesses.

However, further research on Ishtar/Inana/Astarte does not

substantiate the connection between Ishtar and Easter symbols. Ishtar's primary symbol was the star, occasionally the rosette. Her name is similar to the Persian Esther, which means star. The lion served as Ishtar's representative animal. Neither the egg nor the rabbit appears in a dictionary of Mesopotamian symbols.

Hislop points specifically to Astarte for the egg, but further research into Canaanite religion produces no evidence for eggs being associated with Astarte, either. Once again, neither eggs nor rabbits play any role in the religion. The only way to create a link between Ishtar/Astarte and eggs or rabbits is to pull in symbols from other religions. Hislop does this by saying all gods are actually Nimrod and all goddesses are Semiramis. Therefore, if any other goddess has a connection to eggs or rabbits, we can also attribute those symbols to Ishtar.

While scholars accept overlap between various deities, they do not consider them to be interchangeable. No academic material brought all pre-Christian traditions together as one. History does not support an unbroken line from Semiramis through Ishtar and on into Catholicism.

The logic Hislop used to declare these various entities the same is shaky. A simple mention of a god being a hunter is enough to prove that this god is actually Nimrod the mighty hunter by another name. He uses details on illustrations that are recent artist conceptions to prove similarities without noting that they are not from the time period involved.

Nor does he note the amount of time and physical space between some of the customs he uses to prove sameness. He does not consider the possibility historians raise that early people in tune with the agricultural cycle might develop similar customs without an actual link between them.

Another difficulty with Hislop's work is that he assigns motives to people within the Catholic Church that no one can prove now. He believes that the early Catholic leaders adopted paganism intentionally. They were willing to compromise in any way to bring more people within the church. Other materials paint a different picture of how the early church dealt with pagan traditions.

In the end, academic sources do not uphold the contention that Ishtar and Easter are connected. The name Easter has other explanations (see above) and none of the symbols have a direct connection to Ishtar.

The heart of the issue throughout history seems to be what to do with pre-Christian celebrations and customs. Catholic leaders chose to give them Christian meaning and allow people to continue enjoying them. Others, especially during the Reformation era, wanted only what Scripture mentions to be part of faith.

A full discussion of the areas of agreement and disagreement between Protestants and Catholics is beyond the scope of this book. Hislop and others wrote during a period when bloodshed between the two groups was still common – as in some countries today – and the monarch's choice of affiliation could mean life or death to those of the other party.

We face the same issue today, inheriting the choices and arguments from years past. Instead of condemning and calling our brothers and sisters names, perhaps we should focus on Jesus' own desire for His followers: "I do not ask for these only, but also for those who will believe in me through their word, *that they may all be one, just as you, Father, are in me, and I in you,* that they also may be in us, so that the world may believe that you have sent me." John 17:20-21 (emphasis mine).

Easter Symbols and Customs

The Cross

The cross actually pre-dates Christianity. Egyptian and Babylonian monuments long before the time of Christ have crosses carved on them. In fact, early Christians rarely used the cross for the first two centuries following Jesus' death.

Writing around A.D. 200, the Christian Minucius Felix stated, "We Christians neither want nor worship crosses as the pagans do." He did not give a reason, but obviously, some connection existed between the cross and paganism. However, later in the third century, Christians began to use disguised crosses such as the anchor cross, a ship with a mast, or the initials for Jesus and Christ in Greek or Latin superimposed to create a cross-like design.

After Constantine, the cross became an openly Christian symbol during the fourth century. Emperor Theodosius (A.D. 371-395) abolished crucifixion, allowing negative associations with the cross to diminish while it became a symbol of faith.

The original cross may have been what we know as a tau cross, a "T" shape. The word used in the Bible text does not give any clues as to the exact appearance of the cross on which Jesus died. The word simply means "tree" or "stake." The most commonly used form is the Latin cross made of two plain pieces.

Other crosses add additional symbolism to the basic reminder of Jesus' death. For example the "budded" cross with its three small buds on each end suggests the young or immature Christian. The Celtic cross, with its circle around the center arm crossing, adds the symbol of eternity to that of salvation. Many crosses, such as the Jerusalem cross and the Maltese cross, developed during the time of the crusades, when different crusader groups adopted individual styles as a form of identification.

The Easter Bunny

What is the first thing that comes to mind when you think of Easter? As a Christian, the first image might be the cross or the empty tomb. For the general public, a blitz of media images and merchandise on store shelves makes the Easter Bunny more likely. So how did a rabbit distributing eggs become a part of Easter?

The hare and not the rabbit is the original part of the holiday. People across Europe were familiar with the hare and used it in early traditions. The previously mentioned connection between Eostre and the hare gives the first glimpse of the familiar Easter Bunny. Even though scholars don't find evidence for a goddess named Eostre, the hare is still a part of Easter.

We have several reasons to associate the hare with Easter, all of which come through pagan celebrations or beliefs. The most obvious is the hare's fertility. Easter comes during spring and is a celebration of new life. The Christian meaning of new life through Christ and a general emphasis on new life are different, but the two gradually merged. Any animal like the hare that produced many offspring was easy to include.

The hare is also an ancient symbol for the moon. The fact that the date of Easter depends on the moon may have made it easier people to accept the hare as part of Christian Easter celebrations. The hare's connection to the moon is much stronger than to springtime.

The Egyptian name for hare was *un*, meaning open or to open. Hares are born with their eyes open, and Egyptians saw this as another connection with the moon. They mirror the lunar cycle when they carry their young for a month before birth, and they are nocturnal.

The hare or rabbit's burrow helped the animal's adoption as part of Easter celebrations. Believers saw the rabbit coming out of its underground home as a good symbol for Jesus coming out of the tomb. Perhaps this was another case of taking a pre-existing symbol and giving it Christian meaning.

Like many other customs, the Easter rabbit seems to have a German origin. A late sixteenth century German book says, "Do not worry if the bunny escapes you; should we miss his eggs then we shall cook the nest."

In a 1682 German book the bunny lays eggs and hides them in the garden, but even at this date the writers referred to it as an old fable. According to this account, the bunny laid red eggs on Maundy Thursday and the other colors on Easter Eve.

The Easter hare came to America with German immigrants from the Palatine region, and the hare's role passed to the common American rabbit. Originally children made nests for the rabbit in hats, bonnets, or fancy paper boxes, rather than the baskets of today. Then they put the nests in secluded spots to keep from frightening the shy rabbit. The appealing nests full of brightly colored eggs probably helped the custom spread as people from different backgrounds settled in the same area.

Back in Southern Germany, the first pastry and candy Easter bunnies became popular at the beginning of the nineteenth century. This custom also crossed the Atlantic, and children still eat candy rabbits – particularly chocolate ones – at Easter.

Easter Eggs

Next to the Easter bunny, the most familiar symbol of Easter is the Easter egg. Like others, the egg has a long pre-Christian history. Again there's no certainty as to why it became associated with Easter.

Many ancient cultures viewed eggs as a symbol of life, often associated specifically with creation. Egyptians, Persians, Phoenicians, and Hindus believed the world began with an enormous egg. The Persians, Greeks, and Chinese gave gifts of eggs during spring festivals in celebration of new life all around them. Other sources say people ate dyed eggs at spring festivals in Egypt, Persia, Greece, and Rome. In ancient Druid lore, the eggs of serpents were sacred and stood for life.

Early Christians looked at the connection eggs had to life and decided eggs could be a part of their celebration of Christ's resurrection. Seeing a chick hatch from an egg easily became a symbol of life with Christian meaning. Jesus rose from His tomb to bring new life just as an eggshell breaks to release the chick.

In addition, in some areas church rules forbade eating eggs during Lent, and therefore they were a delicacy for Easter. Since many of the earlier customs were Eastern in origin, some speculate that early missionaries or knights of the Crusade may have been responsible for bringing the tradition to the West.

In the fourth century people presented eggs in church to be blessed and sprinkled with holy water. By the twelfth century, the church introduced the *Benedictio Ovorum*, authorizing the special use of eggs on the holy days of Easter. The timing of this blessing upholds the idea that Crusaders may have brought the tradition back from the East with them. Even though people had used eggs previously, the Crusaders may have made the custom more popular and widespread.

In 1290, Edward I of England recorded a purchase of 450 eggs to be colored or covered with gold leaf. He then gave the eggs to members of the royal household.

Pope Paul V, who served between 1605 and 1621, appointed a prayer for use during Mass at Eastertide. "Bless, O Lord, we beseech Thee, this Thy creature of eggs, that it may become a wholesome sustenance to Thy faithful servants, eating in thankfulness to Thee, on account of the Resurrection of Our Lord." The prayer is still a part of Roman Catholic ritual in more modern language.

Once the custom became accepted, new traditions began to grow up around it. People dyed eggs red for joy, and in memory of Christ's blood. Egg rolling contests came to America from England, possibly developed as a reminder of the stone rolled away on Resurrection morning.

What about the familiar Easter egg hunt? One source suggested this grew out of the tradition of German children searching for hidden pretzels during the Easter season. Since children hid nests for the Easter Bunny to fill with eggs at the same time they hunted pretzels, it was only a small leap to begin hiding eggs instead.

Easter Lilies

The Easter lily is another new addition to Easter celebrations. Throughout the years, painters and sculptors used the white Madonna lily to symbolize purity and innocence, frequently referring to Mary. This lily does not force well, so nurseries couldn't get the flower to bloom in time for Easter.

In the 1880s, an amateur gardener, Mrs. Thomas P. Sargent brought Bermuda lily bulbs back to Philadelphia. William K. Harris, a local nurseryman, saw the lilies and introduced them to the trade. A more practical consideration was that they were easy to force into bloom in time for the Easter season. From there, the Bermuda lily, now the familiar Easter lily, spread throughout the country.

Lamb

Of all Easter symbols, the lamb is probably the most strongly Christian. Other than the fact that lambs are young animals born in springtime, it has no strong ties to pagan traditions. The lamb comes from the Jewish Passover, where each family killed a lamb as a sacrifice. John the Baptist first connected Jesus to the Passover lamb when he identified Jesus, saying, "Behold, the Lamb of God, who takes away the sin of the world!" When He died on the cross, Jesus became the Passover Lamb for everyone and the lamb became a symbol for His sacrifice.

New Clothes at Easter

New clothes have long been associated with the idea of newness and a fresh beginning. The familiar custom of having new clothes for Easter probably began with early Christians wearing new white robes for baptism during Easter Vigil services. Later, the custom expanded to everyone wearing new clothes in celebration of his or her new life in Christ.

Sunrise Services

The familiar sunrise service is a relatively new addition to Easter. A group of young Moravian men in Hernhut, Saxony held the first recorded sunrise service in 1732. They went to their cemetery, called God's Acre, at sunrise to worship in memory of the women who went to the tomb early on the first Easter morning and discovered it empty. Moravian immigrants brought the custom to America, with the first service in the U.S. held in 1743.

Via Dolorosa and the Stations of the Cross

Separating the two is difficult, since the Via Dolorosa is the route Jesus may have followed on the way to the cross, and the stations commemorate different events during the trip. The name for the route is Latin for "way of sorrows" or "way of suffering."

The tradition of commemorating the Stations of the Cross probably started when early pilgrims to Jerusalem followed the traditional route Jesus took from Pilate's house to Calvary. Pilgrims continued and popularized the practice through the crusades (1095-1270). After the crusades, Moslems recaptured Israel and pilgrimages were too dangerous.

During this time, various groups within the church built copies of the sepulcher that included markers to represent the events on the way to the cross. These allowed people to share the experience of retracing Jesus' road to the cross without leaving the country and braving the political turmoil in the Middle East.

The Franciscans took the idea one step further during the Middle Ages. They put up wooden crosses in churches to represent the different events. The number of stations still varied, but there were usually about fourteen. Finally, in 1731 Pope Clement XII set the number of stations as the fourteen used today.

The traditional Stations of the Cross mix events recorded in Scripture with later additions. You can find the stations along the actual Via Dolorosa in Jerusalem. Many churches today still set up representations of the stations as devotional helps during Lent and Easter. Within the Catholic Church, a strict set of rules governs how these should be presented..

The Stations of the Cross begin with Christ before Pilate, and end with His crucifixion on Calvary. Those marked with an asterix (*) in this list are events mentioned in Scripture.

1. Jesus is condemned to death *
2. Roman soldiers force Jesus to carry His cross *
3. Jesus falls under the weight of the cross for the first time
4. Jesus meets Mary, His mother
5. Soldiers make Simon of Cyrene carry the cross *
6. Veronica wipes Jesus' face
7. Jesus falls the second time
8. The women of Jerusalem weep for Jesus *
9. Jesus falls the third time
10. Soldiers strip Jesus of his garments *
11. Jesus is nailed to the cross *
12. Jesus dies on the cross *
13. Friends take Jesus down from the cross *

14. Jesus is placed in the tomb *
At times people add a 15th station for the resurrection.

Veronica is one of the legendary additions to the Stations of the Cross, probably French in origin. The legend tells that she offered Jesus her head cloth to wipe His face on His way to the cross. When He returned the veil, she found His features imprinted on it.

Scripture doesn't specifically mention Jesus meeting His mother and falling under the cross. We know that Mary was present at the crucifixion, so an earlier meeting with her was certainly possible. Since the Romans forced Simon of Cyrene to carry Jesus' cross He probably was so weak from the beating that He fell along the way.

PASSOVER

Date varies

"This day shall be for you a memorial day, and you shall keep it as a feast to the LORD; throughout your generations, as a statute forever, you shall keep it as a feast. Exodus 12:14.

Easter and Passover are both floating holidays where the moon determines the celebration date. People may celebrate Passover before, during, or after Easter week. Though some consider Passover a Jewish holy day, Passover and the future Easter joined when Jesus' crucifixion and resurrection took place during Passover.

The Last Supper may have been a Passover meal. Matthew, Mark, and Luke indicate that it was Passover, but John states that it was the Day of Preparation for the Passover. Today Christians are beginning to add the celebration of Passover to Easter, recognizing Easter as completing the redemption foreshadowed by offering the lamb at the first Passover.

In Exodus 12:1-20, God gave specific directions for the Passover feast, as well as directions for the accompanying Feast of Unleavened Bread. People once referred to the entire week including the Feast of Unleavened Bread as Passover. This custom may explain the difference between the four gospels' accounts.

The first Passover occurred when God released the people of Israel from their captivity in Egypt. As the last plague on the Egyptians, God put to death the firstborn of every household. God told the Israelites to kill a lamb and mark their doorways with its blood. When the Angel of Death came, it passed over the homes marked with blood.

Today Passover or Pesah celebrations vary due to factors including orthodox, conservative, and liberal elements within Judaism, different national or regional traditions, and allowed rabbinical variations. Though what follows is an outline of modern Pesah, keep in mind that differences exist.

Celebrating Passover involves three major parts: telling the story of the Exodus, eating *matzah* or unleavened bread, and refraining from either eating or owning *hametz* (anything made with leavening). These parts guide the celebration throughout. The Seder meal provides a format for telling the story of the Exodus and eating matzah, while refraining from *hametz* takes place during preparation.

Before Passover begins, the head of each household must see that the family removes all *hametz* from the home. Depending on how strict you are, this can include everything from a thorough cleaning to owning extra dishes and stoves for use solely during Passover.

Removing *hametz* follows a formula. First the children search for *hametz*, usually a few bits and pieces left where they can easily find them. They bring these to the head of the household for destruction. First, he recites a formula to nullify any remaining *hametz* in the house. In it, he relinquishes ownership of any leavened material not found and removed. After dealing with any extra material, he destroys whatever *hametz* the children found, usually by burning. Then he recites the nullifying formula once again to insure that the house is completely free of leaven and ready for Passover.

The main celebration of Passover focuses on the Seder meal and its accompanying *Haggadah* – a liturgy telling the Exodus story and providing the script for the evening. The Seder plate, *k'areh* in Hebrew, displays symbolic foods for the celebration. People may use a variety of different arrangements of food, and different recipes and substitutes are available for some portions.

The Seder plate contains the following or accepted substitutes:

1. *Karpas* - a vegetable, frequently a green vegetable like parsley, which is dipped in salt water near the beginning of the Seder
2. *Haroset* - a mixture of chopped apples, nuts, wine, and spices symbolizing the mortar for the bricks of slavery
3. *Maror* - bitter herbs such as romaine lettuce or horseradish
4. *Beitzah* - a roasted egg symbolizing the sacrifice all Jews were required to bring to the Temple for Passover.
5. *Zeroa* - a roasted bone, usually a shank bone, symbolizing the Passover lamb sacrifice.

In addition, the leader places three *matzot* near the Seder plate, either stacked on top of each other or placed in a special *matzah* cover with three compartments. During the celebration, everyone must drink four cups of wine or grape juice as a substitute. The celebration also requires salt water to symbolize tears and Elijah's cup, set aside for the prophet's visit during Passover.

In the ancient world, reclining while eating was a symbol of freedom, so reclining to the left for portions of the Passover meal is traditional. When eating the symbols of slavery, participants don't recline. The leader may wear a *kittel,* a white robe similar to priestly garments worn during the Temple service, but this is up to the individual's preference.

As with the foods, the exact order may differ, but a basic outline of the Seder follows.

I. *Kadesh* – the leader recites a blessing over the first cup of wine, which participants drink while reclining.

II. *Ur-hatz* - hand washing and a traditional blessing

III. *Karpas* – participants dip the vegetable in salt water to symbolize the tears shed by the Israelites while they were Egyptian slaves

IV. *Yahatz* - the middle matzah is broken into two unequal pieces; the larger is wrapped and set aside for the *afikomen,* eaten at the end of the meal, while the smaller piece goes back in the cover; the children often "steal" the *afikomen* and hold it for ransom

V. *Maggid* - telling the story of the Exodus, this includes the traditional Four Questions and other Scriptures, commentary, and songs, ending with the second cup of wine

VI. *Rohtzah* - a ritual hand washing and blessing

VII & VIII *Motzi, Matzah* - two blessings, the one for bread and one for matzah; everyone eats from the top and bottom matzot while reclining

IX. *Maror* - bitter herbs dipped in *haroset,* blessed, and eaten upright, not reclining

X. *Koreikh* - bottom matzah eaten as a sandwich with *maror* because the sage Hillel believed participants ate them together during Temple times

XI. *Shulham Oreikh* – participants eat the meal itself; some begin the meal with eggs dipped in salt water

XII. *Tzafun* - *afikomen* is ransomed and eaten while reclining

XIII. *Bareikh* - grace after meals recited and the third cup of wine is blessed and drunk while reclining

XIV. *Hallel* - the door is opened for Elijah and traditional verses are recited, the blessing over wine is recited and the fourth cup drunk while reclining; the blessing after drinking wine is also recited.

XV. *Nirtzah* - the conclusion of the Seder, including part of a poem and reciting or singing "Next year in Jerusalem" and a variety of songs

Different traditions have grown up around Passover through time. Today's Seder plate is of fairly recent origin. The most popular and common arrangement of elements is from a sixteenth century rabbi, Isaac Luria. Other customs are of similarly recent origin: eating hard boiled eggs (sixteen century), ransoming the *afikomen* (seventeen century), and the cup of Elijah (late seventeen century). Christians interested in celebrating Passover can find books translating the Seder into Christian understanding in addition to those from a strictly Jewish perspective.

The Passover is clearly about redemption, and modern Jewish commentators often stress the Messianic nature of Passover. As one said, "Messianic hope would not be credible in the world as we know it were it not for the fact - rehearsed at Pesah - that redemption has occurred." For Christians, of course, Jesus fulfilled Messianic hope at a Passover nearly two thousand years ago.

Because of the changes in how people have celebrated Passover since the Exodus, we can't know for sure which parts of the ceremony God intended to foreshadow Jesus' death. The most obvious parallel is the sacrificial lamb. Scripture is clear about Jesus' identity as the Lamb of God, beginning with John's recognition: "The next day he saw Jesus coming toward him, and said, "Behold, the Lamb of God, who takes away the sin of the world!" John 1:29. The Passover lamb, therefore, was a visible symbol preparing people for the coming of Jesus, who would perform the final sacrifice.

Other ties link Jesus and Passover. Exodus instructed that people should roast the lamb whole. Specifically, no bones were to be broken. When Jesus died on the cross, His legs were not broken, as was common practice at the time, connecting the final Passover Lamb to the instructions in Exodus.

The final tie between Jesus and the Passover lamb came from the cross. "After this, Jesus, knowing that all was now finished, said (to fulfill the Scripture), 'I thirst.' A jar full of sour wine stood there, so they put a sponge full of the sour wine on a hyssop branch and held it to his mouth." John 19:28-29. Much earlier, at the first Passover, God told the Israelites to use the hyssop plant to put lambs' blood on the doorposts. In John the soldiers used hyssop to give Jesus a final drink as He died.

Putting the Last Supper into its context as a Passover Meal is more difficult, since the Gospels do not give us many details. In Luke's account of the meal, he tells us Jesus "took the cup" on two different occasions, which would be consistent with a Passover celebration. The difficulty lies in the fact that the traditional Passover would have included four cups of wine.

Of the four cups, the first and third are the most important, so some sources think Luke mentioned these two cups. The first cup Jesus gives his followers, telling them "I will not drink again of the fruit of the vine until the kingdom of God comes" may have been the first cup of Passover, which traditionally consecrated the meal.

The third cup was the cup of redemption. People drank this cup with a small piece of the *afikoman*. Because participants took the bread and wine together at this point, we can see the parallel to Jesus' institution of the Lord's Supper. Since the third cup represented redemption, the parallel becomes stronger, as Jesus was offering Himself as the redemption for all.

The wine used in the celebration pulls the two more closely together as well. Passover wine should be blood red in color. Jesus' statement, "This cup is the new covenant in my blood, which is poured out for you," is more dramatic in the context of a blood red wine from the cup of redemption.

Modern Jewish commentary underscores the Messianic nature of the Passover. One commentator says the middle matzah, broken during the ceremony, represents the messianic redemption to come. Though we don't know how long this association has been in place, the parallel to Jesus breaking bread and saying "This is my body given for you." Luke 22:19, is fairly obvious as well. Was he breaking a piece of matzah which already symbolized messianic redemption? The action would be consistent with the kind of word-pictures Jesus used in teaching, but we don't know for sure.

Christian author Ray Vander Laan sums up the connection between Passion Week and Passover, as well as other related observances very well. His work clearly illustrates the shadows of the Passion in Jewish festivals. Jesus entered Jerusalem on the day people chose their sacrificial lamb, what we now call Palm Sunday. His death on the cross took place during Passover at the hour of the final sacrifice.

Jesus's friends placed Him in the tomb at the beginning of the Feast of Unleavened Bread. This feast offered God thanks for life as symbolized by bread that He provides. The Resurrection took place on the Feast of Firstfruits, a celebration of the beginning of harvest.

In addition, God sent the Holy Spirit at Pentecost or Shavuot, the second of the three great Jewish feasts. Shavuot was also a harvest celebration, just as Jesus had predicted there would be a great harvest of believers. About three thousand believed on that first Pentecost, and the harvest continues. God provided the feasts to point the way to the fulfillment which came in Jesus' death, burial, and resurrection.

MAY

Sweet child of May you'll taste the caress

of Emerald's promised happiness.

Birthstone: Emerald

Birthstone Virtue: Discovers false friends and insures true love

Flower: Lily of the Valley

As with April, we are uncertain of the name's origin, but it may refer to Maria, goddess of springtime growth. The name could refer to the Majores branch of the Roman senate.

NATIONAL DAY OF PRAYER

Date varies - first Thursday in May

if my people who are called by my name humble themselves, and pray and seek my face and turn from their wicked ways, then I will hear from heaven and will forgive their sin and heal their land. II Chronicles 7:14.

Prayer came to America with the first Puritan settlers, who quickly established it as a part of American life. The Continental Congress issued the first call to national prayer, requesting the colonies to pray for wisdom in forming a nation. President Lincoln followed a familiar tradition when he proclaimed a day of humiliation, fasting, and prayer in 1863.

This background made Congress' joint resolution in 1952 setting a national day of prayer a natural move. President Harry Truman then signed the resolution into law:

"WHEREAS from the earliest days of our history our people have been accustomed to turn to Almighty God for help and guidance; and

WHEREAS in times of national crisis when we are striving to strengthen the foundations of peace and security we stand in special need of divine support; and

WHEREAS I deem it fitting that this Day of Prayer coincide with the anniversary of the adoption of the Declaration of Independence, which published to the world this Nation's 'firm reliance on the protection of Divine Providence':

NOW, THEREFORE, I, HARRY S. TRUMAN, President of the United States of America, do hereby proclaim Friday, July 4, 1952, as a National Day of Prayer, on which all of us, in our churches, in our homes, and in our hearts, may beseech God to grant us wisdom to now the course which we should follow, and strength and patience to pursue that course steadfastly. May we also give thanks to Him for His constant watchfulness over us in every house of national prosperity and national peril.

IN WITNESS WHEREOF, I have hereunto set my hand and caused the Seal of the United States of America to be affixed.

DONE at the City of Washington this seventeenth day of June, in the year of our Lord nineteen hundred and fifty-two, and of the Independence of the United States of America the one hundred and seventy-sixth."

President Ronald Reagan amended the resolution in 1988, changing the day from "a suitable day each year, other than Sunday" to "the first Thursday in May in each year."

Observances vary across the U.S., though the National Day of Prayer Task Force provides materials to guide interested groups in planning services. The day isn't just for Christians, but encourages people from all faiths to join in praying for America.

MOTHER'S DAY

Date varies - second Sunday in May

" 'Honor your father and your mother, as the LORD your God commanded you, Deuteronomy 5:16.

What kind of memories do you have of Mother's Day from your childhood? Was your church one that recognized all mothers in the congregation in some way? Perhaps you remember needing to have the right color corsage for both you and your mother. Somehow May flowers and honoring mothers go together naturally.

While the American holiday is fairly new, the idea of a day set aside to honor mothers is not. Both the ancient Greeks and Romans held festivals to honor mothers. For a more modern example, people in England celebrate the fourth Sunday of Lent as Mothering Sunday.

The roots of the American Mother's Day go back to the Civil War. Julia Ward Howe, author of "Battle Hymn of the Republic" suggested that Americans should rename July fourth as Mother's Day and use the day to promote peace. Her efforts bore no fruit.

After the War, Anna Reeves Jarvis of Grafton, West Virginia organized a committee in 1868 to sponsor a Mother's Friendship Day. Her object was to reunite families divided by the Civil War. She had some success, but the day never spread.

Mary Towles Saseen, a teacher in Henderson, Kentucky organized a special musical affair as a tribute to her pupils' mothers in 1887. It became an annual event and she worked to popularize recognizing mothers at other schools until her death in 1916. Again, though people accepted the idea, it did not spread widely.

Anna M. Jarvis, the daughter of Anna Reeves Jarvis, was most directly responsible for today's celebration. On May 9, 1907, the second anniversary of her mother's death, she invited friends to her home in Philadelphia where she outlined plans for making her mother's dream of a nationwide day honoring mothers a reality.

The next year, on May 10, 1908, churches held services honoring mothers in Grafton, West Virginia, and in Philadelphia. For the service at Andrews Methodist Church in Grafton, Miss Jarvis provided hundreds of carnations, her mother's favorite flower. Each mother and child in attendance received a carnation during the service.

Shortly after the first celebration, Jane Stewart, a lecturer and editor, wrote:

"Large jars of white carnations (the floral emblem of mother-love because of its sweetness, purity, and endurance) are set about the platform. These fragrant flowers may be the gift of those who have lost their mothers or of those who wish in this way to show respect and honor to mothers at a distance. And at the close of the exercise one of these white carnations is given to each person present as an appropriate souvenir of Mother's Day."

Anna M. Jarvis continued working to promote her idea. In 1910, the governor of West Virginia issued the first Mother's Day proclamation. By 1911, churches held Mother's Day services in all states of the Union.

In May 1913, the House of Representatives unanimously passed a resolution asking the President, his Cabinet, the members of both Houses and all officials of the federal government to wear a white carnation on Mother's Day. The House followed with a resolution on May 7, 1914 recommending that the second Sunday in May be designated as Mother's Day. Introduced by Representative James T. Heflin of Alabama and Senator Morris Sheppard of Texas, it passed both Houses.

In response, President Woodrow Wilson issued his Mother's Day Proclamation on May 9, 1914.

WHEREAS, By a Joint Resolution approved May 8, 1914, "designating the second Sunday in May as Mother's Day, and for other purposes," the President is authorized and requested to issue a proclamation calling upon the government officials to display the United States flag on all government buildings, and the people of the United States to display the flag at their homes or other suitable places on the second Sunday in May as a public expression of our love and reverence for the mothers of our country:

AND WHEREAS, By the said Joint Resolution it is made the duty of the President to request the observance of the second Sunday in May as provided for in the said Joint Resolution:

Now, Therefore, I, Woodrow Wilson, President of the United States of America, by virtue of the authority vested in me by the said Joint Resolution, do hereby direct the government officials to display the United States flag on all government buildings and do invite the people of the United States to display the flag at their homes or other suitable places on the second Sunday in May as a public expression of our love and reverence for the mothers of our country."

The custom of wearing carnations continued and gradually changed with red carnations a symbol of a living mother and white ones for mothers who had died. Though the symbolism was the same, people in the rural South used roses instead of carnations. This was a matter of practicality, not refusal to conform. With little money and few florists, people didn't have access to carnations, but roses bloomed in gardens everywhere during May.

Following an exhibit of the painting of James Whistler's mother by Chicago's Century of Process Exposition of 1934, the U.S. postal service issued a stamp of the painting in honor of Mother's Day.

As commercialism began to creep into the celebration, Anna M. Jarvis became embittered and even initiated lawsuits against those seeking profits from Mother's Day. Ironically, though she spent her entire life working to honor mothers, she never married and had no children. She died in 1948.

Andrews Methodist Church, where congregants held the first Mother's Day service, is now the International Mother's Day Shrine, which is open to the public.

MEMORIAL DAY

May 30th

For everything there is a season, and a time for every matter under heaven: a time to be born, and a time to die . . . a time for war, and a time for peace. Ecclesiastes 3:1-2,8.

Nearly all cultures have customs to honor the dead. The Greeks held a March Commemoration of the Dead, while the Romans decorated graves with flowers to celebrate Parentalia. The Roman celebration in some ways resembled many held at churches today. The observance became a family reunion where members offered wine, milk, honey, oil, and water at the flower decorated graves and ended with a family feast. A Roman might feel at home at a modern Memorial Day service with dinner on the grounds.

These older festivals were usually seasonal occurrences. Often they tied in to New Year's celebrations where the dead could move back into the world of the living as part of the chaos of the year's change.

By contrast, our modern Memorial Day dates back to the Civil War. In the early days, people often referred to the time as Decoration Day since a major part of the ceremony was decorating the graves with flowers. Though usually called Memorial Day now, decorating graves is still a part of the observance.

History offers a variety of possible contenders for the title of first Memorial Day. Most likely people in the South held the first informal Memorials before the end of the War. Many of the war dead lay buried in the South, the scene of most of the fighting.

The official holder of the title of "first Memorial Day" is Waterloo, New York. Druggist Henry C. Welles suggested the celebration and Union general John B. Murray approved it. He also gathered support from veterans and formed a committee to plan the ceremonies. The town honored its war dead on May 5, 1866. Businesses closed for the day, flags flew at half mast, and black mourning draperies mixed with evergreen boughs hung throughout the town. Veterans, civic, and fraternal groups paraded to the three local cemeteries, where General Murray and the Reverend Dr. Samuel Gridley spoke.

Many years later, on March 7, 1966, Governor Nelson Rockefeller proclaimed Waterloo the original site of Memorial Day. Congressman Samuel S. Stratton of New York then introduced a resolution in the House of Representatives. The resolution passed the House on May 17 and the Senate approved it on May 19. President Lyndon B. Johnson then issued a proclamation officially recognizing Waterloo as the "birthplace of Memorial Day." In response, the community dedicated the Waterloo Memorial Day Museum on May 30, 1967. The Museum contains relics from the 1866 celebration and Civil War memorabilia.

Boalsburg, Pennsylvania is another leading contender for the honor of hosting the first Memorial Day. On an October Sunday in 1864 Emma Hunter went to the cemetery to put flowers on the grave of her father, Colonel James Hunter. There she met Mrs. Meyer who was doing the same for her son. They agreed to meet the next year to decorate the graves again. The custom spread and was established by May 30, 1869.

In Vicksburg, Mississippi, Sue Langdon Vaughan and others decorated the graves of those who had fallen before the end of the siege of Vicksburg. The ceremony there took place on April 26, 1865. The cemetery is now part of the Vicksburg National Military Park.

One of the best publicized of the early Memorials took place at Columbus, Mississippi on April 25, 1866. Men killed at the Battle of Shiloh and those who died in the Columbus Military Hospital lay buried at the Friendship Cemetery. A group of women began tending the graves of Confederate soldiers in early spring, which inspired other women to join them for the April 25th memorial.

Young girls dressed in white led the procession to the cemetery. Wives and widows dressed in black followed, with older participants in carriages. At the cemetery everyone formed a square around the graves, and listened to a prayer and a commemorative speech before placing the flowers on the graves. After placing flowers on the Confederate graves, the women turned spontaneously and put magnolia blossoms on the graves of the Union soldiers also buried there.

News of their action spread and was picked up by Horace Greeley's New York Tribune. He wrote:

"The women of Columbus, Mississippi, have shown themselves impartial in their offerings to the memory of the dead. They strewed flowers alike on the graves of the Confederate and of the National soldiers."

An attorney in Ithaca, New York, Francis Miles Finch, responded to the account with a poem in the September 1867 issue of the Atlantic Monthly. Many newspapers reprinted the poem, "The Blue and the Gray," and students across the country memorized it. The poem reads in part:

"By the flow of the inland river,
When the fleets of iron have fled,
Where the blades of the grave grass quiver,
Asleep are the ranks of the dead;
Under the sod and the dew,
Waiting the judgment day;
Under the one, the Blue;
Under the other, the Gray. . . .

From the silence of sorrowful hours
The desolate mourners go,
Lovingly laden with flowers
Alike for the friend and the foe;
Under the sod and the dew,
Waiting the judgment day;
Under the roses, the Blue;
Under the lilies, the Gray. . . .

Sadly, but not with upbraiding,
The generous deed was done;
In the storm of the years that are fading
No braver battle was won;
Under the sod and the dew,
Waiting the judgment day;
Under the blossoms, the Blue;
Under the garlands, the Gray."

In turn the publicity helped to heal the breach between North and South following the end of the Civil War. People from the South began to travel north to decorate the graves of loved ones while people in the North traveled south to do the same. Shared grief and respect helped during the difficult post-War years.

An organization of Union veterans, the Grand Army of the Republic, suggested May 30 as a national Memorial Day in 1866. An unknown Union soldier from Ohio wrote suggesting an annual memorial. We don't know his name, but we know he was of German origin. He may not have heard of the Columbus ceremony and probably patterned his suggestion after *Heldengedenktag*, "Heroes' Memory Day," celebrated in Germany on March 12.

His suggestion met with approval, and General John A. Logan, commander in chief, recommended arrangements be made to decorate the graves of Union soldiers throughout the country. He issued an order to all Grand Army posts:

"The thirtieth day of May, 1868, is designated for the purpose of strewing with flowers or otherwise decorating the graves of comrades who died in defense of their country during the late rebellion, and whose bodies now lie in almost every city, village and hamlet churchyard in the land."

He did not dictate any particular type of ceremony, but left the details up to each individual post to determine. This allowed for a more personal touch at each separate location. The original dispatch states clearly he intended the remembrance to be a yearly occurrence as long as a "survivor of the war remains to honor the memory of his departed comrades."

General Logan called on the press to help spread the word about the celebration throughout the country so that everyone would hold observances on the same day. He instructed departmental commanders to use every effort to make the order effective.

As a result, groups held more than 100 different ceremonies. At the National Cemetery in Arlington, Virginia, Ulysses S. Grant attended and General James A. Garfield spoke, saying in part:

"I am oppressed with a sense of the impropriety of uttering words on this occasion. If silence is ever golden, it must be here beside the graves of fifteen thousand men whose lives were more significant than speech and whose death was a poem the music of which can never be sung."

After 1868, Memorial Day observances multiplied throughout the nation. New York was the first state to designate May 30th a legal holiday in 1873, followed by Rhode Island in 1874, Vermont in 1876, New Hampshire in 1877, Wisconsin in 1879, and Massachusetts and Ohio in 1881. By 1890 it had become a legal holiday in all of the northern states.

Memorial Day is now a legal holiday in all fifty states, though some of the Southern states still celebrate older Confederate anniversaries in addition to Memorial Day. Since June 28, 1968, when

President Lyndon Johnson signed legislation moving the dates of holidays to provide more three-day weekends, Americans have observed Memorial Day on the last Monday of May each year.

Why originators chose May 30th is uncertain. Perhaps proximity to the May 26, 1865 surrender of the last Confederate Army by General Kirby-Smith on influenced the choice. The return of peace at the end of May made it a logical time to remember those who fell during the War.

As America fought other wars after the Civil War, Memorial Day became a time to honor victims of each additional war as well. Official ceremonies still remember the war dead, but Memorial Day has now become a time to remember all those who have gone before, not just those who died in wars.

JUNE

Pearls for the girls of June, the precious wealth,

and to crown it all they bring her health.

Birthstone: Pearl, Moonstone

Birthstone Virtue: Wealth

Flower: Rose

Juno, Roman goddess of marriage and women, provided the name for June.

PENTECOST

Date varies - May/June

*And suddenly there came from heaven a sound like a mighty
rushing wind, and it filled the entire house where they were
sitting. And divided tongues as of fire appeared to them and
rested on each one of them. And they were all filled with
the Holy Spirit and began to speak in other tongues as the
Spirit gave them utterance. Acts 2:2-4*

You may be familiar with Pentecost as the time at which the Holy
Spirit came to the first believers after Christ's ascension. The name
comes from the Greek *pentekoste* or "the fiftieth," referring to the fifty
days from Passover to this day. The focus of the day is the descent of
the Holy Spirit, but it also marks the Christian community's first
assembly. We can call Pentecost the Christian church's birthday.

Early Christians linked Pentecost and Easter so closely that the
period from Easter to Pentecost was one season of rejoicing. Joy has
always been such a major part of this celebration that the Council of
Nicaea outlawed both kneeling and fasting during Pentecost as being
too penitential.

You still might see the names Whitsun or Whitsunday for
Pentecost. In Britain, many people once received baptism on this day.
This may have been because Pentecost was part of the Easter season,
or for the more practical reason that the streams and rivers had warmed
enough for outdoor baptisms. They called the day "White Sunday,"

from the new converts' baptismal robes, and the name became contracted into Whitsunday.

People made Pentecost a major celebration during the Middle Ages. They used a wooden, painted Holy Ghost Dove, white against a blue background with golden rays. During the service a "Holy Ghost Hole" the size of a wagon wheel opened in the ceiling and the Dove swung in circles as it descended over the congregation. In some services, people dropped red roses for the tongues of fire and water for baptism over the congregation.

In a few churches, people dropped burning straw balls from the ceiling to represent the tongues of fire. They suspended this custom for obvious reasons. Members of the congregation blazed with fire outside rather than with the inward fire of the Spirit. In other churches, particularly in France, trumpets called to mind the rushing of the wind when the Spirit came.

Though churches discontinued the older customs, many churches still use red, like the roses used in earlier years, as the liturgical color for Pentecost. Tongues of fire are a symbol of Pentecost, as is the descending dove.

SHAVUOT

Date varies - May/June

You shall keep the Feast of Harvest, of the firstfruits of your labor, of what you sow in the field. Exodus 23:16

Had you been a first century Jewish Christian, you would have known Pentecost as Shavuot or the Feast of Weeks. At the time, people often used the term Pentecost for the entire fifty days preceding the actual day of celebration, a practice the early Christians continued. The alternate term, "Feast of Weeks," came from the fact that people figured the day by counting seven weeks after Pesach.

Shavuot was one of the three "Pilgrim festivals" in Biblical Judaism: Pesach in spring, then Shavuot, and Sukkot in autumn. The Law required a Jewish man to appear in Jerusalem with a festival offering. Shavuot marked the end of the grain harvest and the beginning of the next agricultural season when the fruit began to ripen. During the one-day celebration, priests offered two loaves of leavened bread in the temple as a thanksgiving to God and a prayer for a successful harvest.

During the latter part of the first century, after the fall of Jerusalem in 70 A.D., Pentecost began to change. Without the temple, people could no longer hold the celebration as before. During that time, Shavuot began to celebrate God giving the Torah or Law on Mount Sinai.

The main theme for Shavuot became the covenant between God and the people of Israel, particularly Israel's acceptance of God's Law and His protection. In some commentaries, people see this as a marriage between God and Israel. Moses broke the first set of Ten Commandments because Israel worshiped the golden calf. If he had delivered this first set, Israel would have been committing adultery with another god. The covenant marriage between God and Israel finalized when Moses delivered the Law later.

Over the years, new customs arose to celebrate Shavuot, including decorating with green plants, branches, and trees and eating dairy foods. No one knows for certain where these customs started, though using plants may be a remembrance of the first fruits once brought to the Temple. Focusing on the Law may explain eating dairy foods. One commentator said that eating dairy products and then meat – normally eaten at festivals – remembers the two loaves of the previous offering. Others eat dairy foods with honey because the Law is like milk and honey.

Modern Judaism still celebrates Shavuot. On many kibbutzim in Israel, people hold various religious and secular celebrations of the first fruits similar to the original observance. They have processions and dance and sing to celebrate the fruits of the land.

Reform Jews celebrate confirmation on Shavuot, a tradition borrowed from Christianity. They feel that an individual isn't fully prepared to accept the responsibilities of adulthood at the traditional age of thirteen for the Bar Mitzvah. In some cases, confirmation supplements the Bar Mitzvah and in others takes the place of it. During confirmation boys and girls in their late teens accept the responsibilities of following Jewish tradition and become full adult members of their congregations.

FATHER'S DAY

Date varies - third Sunday in June

"Honor your father and mother" (this is the first commandment with a promise), Ephesians 6:2.

Looking at Father's Day from a modern perspective, you might think having a day for fathers is logical if you're going to have one for mothers. A look at history shows a different story. Mother's Day inspired Father's Day, but Father's Day took more time to catch on.

Central Church of Fairmont, West Virginia celebrated the first Father's Day. Mrs. Charles Clayton suggested the observance to her pastor, Dr. Robert T. Webb. He agreed, and the church held a service to honor fathers on July 5, 1908.

Despite this, people usually credit Sonora Louise Smart Dodd of Spokane, Washington with originating the idea in 1909, because the observance spread beyond her church. Her inspiration for a day to honor fathers came from the already existing Mother's Day and her own father. William Smart, a Civil War veteran, had lost his wife in childbirth and raised his daughter and five sons alone.

Mrs. Dodd saw the celebration as centered on the church, so she discussed the idea with her minister, Dr. Rasmus. He approved of the idea and helped her take it to Rev. Conrad Bluhm, president of the Spokane Ministerial Association, and the Spokane Minister's Alliance. The city's YMCA also agreed to help sponsor the celebration.

The Mayor of Spokane released a Father's Day Proclamation, as did the Governor of Washington, M. E. Hay. Mrs. Dodd would have preferred June 5, her father's birthday, for the first observance, but the date did not leave enough time to plan festivities. Therefore, they held the celebration on the third Sunday, June, 19, 1910, still within his birth month.

The organizers took part of their observance from Mother's Day, with single red roses worn for living fathers and single white ones for fathers who had passed away. Mrs. Dodd's efforts to honor fathers received newspaper coverage throughout the nation. In fact, William Jennings Bryan, an orator and political leader, endorsed her idea formally.

President Woodrow Wilson declined to issue a proclamation supporting or establishing Father's Day, but he did approve of the idea. In 1916 he took part in a Father's Day celebration in Spokane by pushing a button at his desk in Washington which unfurled a flag in Spokane.

Still, the idea was slow to spread. Two years after the first Spokane celebration, in 1912, another city, Vancouver, held a celebration at the suggestion of Rev. J. H. Berringer, pastor of the Irvington Methodist Church. Later, at least one newspaper account showed that the people of Vancouver believed their celebration was the first.

Across the country, other people had the same idea independently. As early as 1915, Harry C. Meek, president of the Uptown Lions Club of Chicago began working to establish Father's Day. He arranged a celebration in 1920, which happened to have been the third Sunday in June, as this was the Sunday nearest his birthday, June 25th.

Katherine Lawrence, later K. L. Burgess, as a teenager in Drewry's Bluff, Virginia wrote a letter to the newspaper in an effort to begin honoring fathers nearly a decade after the Spokane celebrations. In 1921 she persuaded the governor of Virginia to proclaim a Father's Day and registered the name National Father's Day Association with the U. S. Patent office. However, when she heard of the earlier observances in Spokane, she withdrew any claim of being the first to promote the idea.

The idea continued to spread, but was still slow to be declared an official holiday. President Calvin Coolidge refused to proclaim Father's Day, but recommended that all states note the day. Most state governors began to proclaim the third Sunday of June as Father's Day each year.

Senator Margaret Chase Smith was a major proponent of designating an official Father's Day. She made a proposal on February 18, 1957 which read in part:

"As far as I can gather, it seems that the Congress has been guilty now for forty years of the worst possible oversight, to say the least, perpetrated against the gallant fathers, young and old, of our land."

She insisted that singling out only one parent for honor, rather than recognizing both, was an insult. She also suggested that Congress was at fault in not choosing to honor fathers before this time. Finally, in 1972 President Richard Nixon signed a Congressional resolution fixing the day permanently.

The ruby stole a spark from heaven above,

to bring the July maiden fervent Love.

Birthstone: Ruby

Birthstone Virtue: Insures forgetfulness or cure of any ills arising from love or friendship

Flower: Larkspur

As mentioned in the previous information about the calendar, the Roman Senate named July for Julius Caesar.

INDEPENDENCE DAY

July 4th

Blessed is the nation whose God is the LORD, the people whom he has chosen as his heritage! Psalm 33:12.

You're probably familiar with the story of our nation's struggle for independence from Great Britain. Many history books chronicle the details, so we don't need to repeat them here. However, you may find a few additions interesting. In 1777, the year immediately following the adoption of the Declaration of Independence on July 4, many leaders thought July 2 was the logical date to remember.

Richard Henry Lee had brought the issue of independence before the Continental Congress on June 7, 1776. Attending as a delegate from Virginia, Lee had the support of John Adams in advancing his motion:

"Resolved, that these United Colonies are, and of right ought to be, free and independent States, that they are absolved from all allegiance to the British Crown, and that all political connection between them and the State of Great Britain is, and ought to be, totally dissolved."

During the debate over the resolution, Congress appointed a committee to draft a declaration of independence. On July 2, the Lee Resolution passed Continental Congress, thereby dissolving ties with Great Britain and establishing American independence. The Declaration itself was a more formal statement of the intent of the Lee

Resolution.

Philadelphia celebrated independence in 1777 on July 2 with bells, bonfires, and fireworks. Sailors fired salutes from ships in the harbor and people placed candles in the windows of their houses. Congress adjourned for the day, as it has for Independence Day celebrations since. The next year, in 1778, the day changed to July 4. Dr. David Ramsay of Charleston, South Carolina claimed to have delivered the first Fourth of July speech. In years following, speeches and addresses became the focal point of most celebrations.

The first overseas celebration of America's Independence occurred at a dinner party in Paris, France, on July 4, 1778. According to John Adam's diary:
"The Anniversary of the Declaration of American Independence. We had the Honour of the Company of all the American Gentlemen and Ladies, in and about Paris to dine, with Dr. Franklin and me, at Passi, together with a few of the French gentlemen in the neighborhood. . . ."

Massachusetts became the first state officially to recognize Independence Day in 1781. Other states gradually adopted the celebration, which then moved westward with the nation's expansion.

In an odd twist, on the fiftieth anniversary of American Independence, July 4, 1826, both Thomas Jefferson and John Adams died. Five years later, on July 4, 1831, James Monroe died. People at the time saw the deaths of the early leaders on the anniversary of independence as significant.

AUGUST

The August maiden with sweet simplicity

wears sardonyx, gem of felicity.

Birthstone: Sardonyx, Peridot

Birthstone Virtue: Married happiness

Flower: Gladiolus

Augustus Caesar gave his name to August.

SEPTEMBER

Out of the depths shall sapphires come

brings September's child wisdom.

Birthstone: Sapphire

Birthstone Virtue: Frees from enchantment, repentance

Flower: Aster

From the days when September was the seventh month in the calendar, we get the name from the Latin *septem* or seven.

Susan E. Richardson

LABOR DAY

Date varies - 1st Monday in September

Therefore, my beloved brothers, be steadfast, immovable, always abounding in the work of the Lord, knowing that in the Lord your labor is not in vain. I Corinthians 15:58.

After the Civil War, labor became a growing problem in the United States. Most laborers had little contact with management and no one to help them when disputes came up. Owners and managers had no concept of fair treatment for their workers. The combination of being out of touch with, in many cases, callous treatment led workers to organize and form labor unions.

The idea of a specific day for labor followed. In 1882 Peter J. McGuire first proposed setting aside a day to honor labor at an early labor organization meeting, the Brotherhood of Carpenters and Joiners. He shared his idea on a wider scale on May 8, 1882 during a meeting of the New York Central Labor Union.

Part of his idea included the date. He suggested the first Monday in September because "it would come at the most pleasant season of the year, nearly midway between the Fourth of July and Thanksgiving, and would fill a wide gap in the chronology of legal holidays." He also proposed a street parade to "show the strength and esprit de corps of the trade and labor organizations" and suggested ending the day with a picnic or similar type of activity.

The Central Labor Union approved his idea enthusiastically, and people celebrated the first Labor Day in New York City on September 5, 1882. This was a Tuesday, but they changed the observance to the recommended Monday within two years.

The activities of the day closely resembled McGuire's original plan. Ten thousand workers marched up Broadway from City Hall to Union Square, carrying banners and escorted by bands. At the end of the march, participants went to Reservoir Park for a picnic, concert, and speeches. The New York Herald reported on the event:

"Fellow workers and their families sat together, joked together and caroused together. . . . Americans, English, Irish, and Germans. . . hobnobbed as though the common cause had established closer brotherhood."

The idea quickly gained acceptance. Only two years later, in 1884, the future AFL, the Federation of Organized Trades and Labor Unions, endorsed the idea, and groups celebrated in cities throughout the Northeast. By 1895, events took place across the nation.

Oregon was the first state to recognize Labor Day as a legal holiday on February 21, 1887. They set aside the first Saturday in June until 1893 when lawmakers moved the celebration to the first Monday in September. The same year Oregon recognized Labor Day, New Jersey approved the first Monday in September as Labor Day on April 8. New York followed shortly when it approved the day on May 6. Other states adopting the day the same year included Colorado and Massachusetts.

By 1893 twenty more states had established Labor Day. The same year, Congress considered a bill to establish Labor Day as a national holiday. Both houses unanimously approved the bill in 1894. President Grover Cleveland signed an act on June 28, 1894, making it a legal holiday for federal employees and the District of Columbia. Eventually, all remaining states and Puerto Rico legalized the holiday.

From its beginnings in organized labor, Labor Day now honors all who work. It has become more of a family festival, providing a last celebration before the end of summer or one last getaway before settling down to school in the fall.

ROSH HASHANAH

Date varies - September/October

"Speak to the people of Israel, saying, In the seventh month, on the first day of the month, you shall observe a day of solemn rest, a memorial proclaimed with blast of trumpets, a holy convocation. Leviticus 23:24.

Many think of Rosh Hashanah as the Jewish New Year, but this is a more recent idea. Scripture designates this as a day of rest (see Lev. 23:24), but the Bible gives few details about this holiday. Over the years, people tied the celebration of Rosh Hashanah to the creation of the world in addition to a new year.

Rosh Hashanah comes at the beginning of a month with two major holidays: the Day of Atonement (Yom Kippur) and the Feast of Booths (Sukkot). It is also the first of ten penitential days ending with Yom Kippur. The combined focus lent itself well to a New Year focus.

Unlike most other Jewish holidays, people celebrate Rosh Hashanah mostly in the synagogue rather than the home. They celebrate God's kingship as well as His Judgment. In one tradition, on this day God remembers all his creatures and judges people. He opens three different books that record everyone's deeds. One book is for those who are completely wicked. One is for those who are completely righteous. The third is for those in between.

God seals the righteous for life and the wicked for death. He suspends judgment for the middle group until Yom Kippur. During the month of Elul before Rosh Hashanah a traditional greeting is, "May you be inscribed for a good and sweet year." Some may add "May you be inscribed and sealed for a good life" between Rosh Hashanah and Yom Kippur. Others avoid this after the first night of Rosh Hashanah to keep from suggesting that anyone might not already be inscribed.

Blowing the shofar – or ram's horn trumpet – is the only part of the celebration specifically mentioned in the Scripture. Meditations or verses called *piyyutim* are popular during the observance of Rosh Hashanah. In keeping with the theme of the holiday, most focus on the power of God:

"Now he became supreme King of Israel
Mighty and exalted, supreme over all,
Fulfilling what he says, shelter and stronghold,
Lofty and uplifting, enthroner of kings,
He shall reign supreme and forever. . .

Opening his hand, he feeds all the living.
He collects water, slowly to drench parched lands
Day unto day pours forth and declares his praise,
He shall reign supreme and forever."

Rabbi Kalonymos ben Meshullam of Mainz, a famous liturgical poet of the eleventh century wrote one of the best known *piyyutim*.

"The great shofar is sounded;
A gentle whisper is head:
The angels, quaking with fear declare,
'The day of judgment is here
to bring the hosts of heaven to judgment!'
Indeed even they are not guiltless in thy sight.
All mankind passes before thee like a flock of sheep.
As a shepherd seeks out his flock,
making his sheep pass under his rod,
so dost thou make all the living souls pass before thee;
thou dost count and number thy creatures,
fixing their lifetime and inscribing their destiny."

YOM KIPPUR

Date varies - September/October

And this shall be a statute forever for you, that atonement may be made for the people of Israel once in the year because of all their sins." And Aaron did as the LORD commanded Moses. Leviticus 16:34.

Yom Kippur – the Day of Atonement – is the holiest day in the Jewish calendar. The day is one of fasting and repentance, considered to be the "Sabbath of Sabbaths." God set aside Yom Kippur for the people of Israel and gave Moses the celebration's details in Leviticus 16. He covered every aspect, from Aaron's dress to how he should present the sacrifices, and ending with sending the scapegoat into the wilderness.

The service consisted of three major confessions of sin. First, the high priest confessed sin and made atonement for himself and his household. Then he did the same for the community of priests. Finally, he offered confession and sought atonement for the entire Jewish people. The ritual of the scapegoat accompanied this final act.

After the destruction of the temple, priests could no longer carry out the Day of Atonement as set forth in Scripture. The focus began to shift more to individual repentance. Today's synagogue ceremony, *Avodah* or "sacrificial service" describes the high priest's former service.

People today include the souls of the dead in the celebration. Many visit cemeteries. Traditional Jews light two candles, one for the living and one for the dead. Services include a special *Yizkor* "He will remember" service in memory of the dead and end with the confession of faith and blowing the shofar.

After Yom Kippur ends, the special break-the-fast dinner may include traditional foods such as challah, chicken soup, wine, honey or sponge cake, and *taglach* - a sweet pastry containing nuts, honey, and cinnamon.

SUKKOT

And you shall take on the first day the fruit of splendid trees, branches of palm trees and boughs of leafy trees and willows of the brook, and you shall rejoice before the LORD your God seven days. You shall celebrate it as a feast to the LORD for seven days in the year. It is a statute forever throughout your generations; you shall celebrate it in the seventh month. You shall dwell in booths for seven days. All native Israelites shall dwell in booths, Leviticus 23:40-42.

If you could visit Israel when people still worshipped in the temple, as autumn approached you would hear people speaking of "the Festival." People commonly referred to Sukkot, the third of the pilgrim feasts, as if it were the only one. Since Sukkot was one of the most important celebrations of the year, everyone would know which festival you meant.

People also called Sukkot the Feast of Booths or Feast of Tabernacles. Following the penitential nature of Yom Kippur, the mood switches to one of rejoicing at Sukkot. The Jewish term *sukkot* is the plural of *sukkah* or booth.

Celebrating Sukkot comes in three parts: 1) the commandment to live in *sukkot* or booths for seven days; 2) gathering together the fruit and branches; and 3) rejoicing during the holiday. (See Lev 23:40-42)

Joy is such a part of the holiday that rabbis forbid anything that might take away from the general rejoicing. While God commanded living in booths, over the years rabbis have added regulations to make sure the time is not a burden. For example, should the weather turn rainy, people are required, not just allowed, to leave the booth. Everything insures a time of gladness.

A *sukkah* must be a true booth, not lower than five feet or higher than thirty feet. People may use only leaves or straw for the roof. This gives some shade from the sun but still allows the sky to show through. Celebrants must build a new *sukkah* and not adapt it from an existing structure.

According to one source, the booth's fragility symbolized the brevity and insecurity of human life. The booth also reminded them of the time they spent wandering in the wilderness, and how dependent they are on God. Also, living in booths emphasized the equality of all people before God.

Another part of the celebration requires using the branches of different trees to rejoice before the Lord. The traditional plants used are now citron, a palm branch, a sprig of myrtle, and a willow branch. People shake the four together in the four directions, as well as upwards and downwards.

We have a variety of interpretations for using these four species. Some tie the plants to prayer for rain. Others say the four species represent the four Patriarchs: Abraham, Isaac, Jacob, and Joseph.

The Midrash explains that the citron, with both taste and aroma, stands for Jews who both know the Torah and do good deeds. The date growing on the palm has taste but no aroma, and represents Jews who know the Torah but don't perform good deeds. The myrtle has aroma but no taste, so it represents Jews who do good deeds but don't know the Torah. Last, the willow has neither taste nor aroma, and the Jews it represents neither know the Torah nor do good deeds.

During the Temple era, water was a major focus of the celebration, in addition to thanks for the harvest. On the evening of the first day, a ceremony called *Simhat-Bet-Ha-Shoevah* or "Rejoicing at the Water Well" took place. Priests lit a huge candelabrum in the Court of Women, while "men of piety and good works" danced before the lights.

Levites stood on the 15 steps leading from the Court of Women to the Court of Israel playing instruments. At dawn, two priests sounded trumpets, advanced to the eastern gate, then turned to the west and said, "Our fathers when they were in this place turned their backs toward the Temple, and their faces toward the East and worshipped the rising sun, but as for Us, our eyes are turned to the Lord."

On the last day of the ancient celebration, a water offering took place. A priest filled a golden vessel at the Pool of Siloam and carried it in procession to the Temple altar. There he transferred the water to a silver container and poured it on the altar through a spout. He then offered a prayer for rain.

It was probably during this offering that "On the last day of the feast, the great day, Jesus stood up and cried out, "'If anyone thirsts, let him come to me and drink. Whoever believes in me, as the Scripture has said, "Out of his heart will flow rivers of living water.""" John 7:37-38. At a time when the People of Israel were praying for rain, Jesus offered Himself as Living Water.

OCTOBER

October's child in darkness oft may grope,

the iridescent opal bids it hope.

Birthstone: Opal, Tourmaline

Birthstone Virtue: Misfortune and Hope

Flower: Calendula

October's name also comes from its former position in the calendar. The Latin *octo* means eight.

CLERGY APPRECIATION DAY

Date varies - second Sunday in October

*We ask you, brothers, to respect those who labor among you
and are over you in the Lord and admonish you, and to esteem
them very highly in love because of their work.*
I Thessalonians 5:12-13

Clergy Appreciation Day is one of the newest holidays, but has grown explosively during its short lifetime. Though Paul makes it clear in Thessalonians Christians are to honor their leaders, organized efforts to honor clergy only came recently. The idea grew out of a "Pastor of the Year" contest in 1991 held by Under His Wing ministries, led by Jerry Frear. He designed the contest to help congregations focus on good things about their pastor and avoid the "armchair quarterback" syndrome on Monday mornings.

When USA Radio picked up the contest, participants turned in over 200 last minute essays. The contest's response led the ministry to consider more ways to show pastors appreciation. During a brainstorming session, Frear noticed Groundhog Day on the calendar. He thought that if we have a day for groundhogs, we should have one for clergy as well.

The following year, in 1992, they announced the first Pastor's Appreciation Day. Attempts for a presidential declaration failed, but Frear wrote ten states to request state declarations. Eight out of the ten responded, and one hundred ten churches held celebrations.

The second year, 1993, twenty-one states declared Clergy Appreciation Day and thirty thousand churches participated. Articles about the observance appeared in sixteen magazines and thirty-four interviews aired on Christian Radio.

Frear approached Focus on the Family the first year, but they declined to participate then. Later they called back and asked about the possibility of changing the title from "Pastor Appreciation" to "Clergy Appreciation." They also wanted to expand the celebration from a day to a weekend. Because it is easier to get a day declared a holiday than longer period of time, Frear agreed to the title change but not the focus of the celebration.

In 1994 Focus on the Family went on to promote Clergy Appreciation for the entire month of October, though they do recommend the second weekend of the month for churches that prefer a single weekend. In addition, Focus prepared a 20 page planning guide to help congregations plan their celebrations. That first year, churches requested twenty six thousand copies, marking the highest level of response for any promotion in their history.

Dayspring Cards joined the effort in 1995 by creating a thirty card line for clergy and their spouses. They also provided Christian retailers with point of purchase signage, bag stuffers, a store information package, and a poster, giving stores more information about the day and supplying them with tools to support the celebration.

Focus on the Family took things a step further in 1996 with the publication of Pastor's Family, a magazine designed to support pastoral families. Another offering that year was a weekly faxed pastor's newsletter including news summaries and encouragement. Other support materials for pastors include a bimonthly audiocassette series featuring Christian pastors, authors and teachers speaking on various subjects pertaining to pastoral ministry, a Pastoral Ministries team that travels across the country offering seminars and meeting with ministers, a directory of reference materials, and a pastoral care phone line.

The observance has continued to grow. Attempts to have a national day proclaimed have failed, but forty-nine out of the fifty states now declare the second Sunday of October to be Clergy Appreciation Day. Approximately one third of the nation's churches take part every year. In 1998 Australia held the first celebration abroad.

So why all this fuss over recognizing our clergy? Consider these statistics about the nation's clergy:

90% work more than 46 hours per week - the average is 50-75 hours a week

90% feel inadequately trained to cope with job demands

80% feel their ministry has a negative effect on their family

75% experienced a significant stress-related crisis at least once in their ministry

70% have a lower self-image than when they began their ministry

70% do not have someone they consider a close friend

50% feel unable to meet the demands of the job

50% have considered leaving the ministry within the past three months

40% experience a serious conflict with a parishioner at least once a month

Many are on call twenty-four hours a day, seven days a week. They handle spiritual, emotional and physical needs of their parishioners and the community. They often have little time to themselves and subject their families to constant public scrutiny as well as standards higher than those of the average person.

Clergy appreciation has existed informally for years. Scripture makes it clear that doing so is both appropriate and required of us as church members. The recent push to honor clergy is unusual in that no one person or group "owns" the holiday. Three different ministries are working in their own way and yet are pulling together under God's guidance to recognize our hardworking clergy.

HALLOWEEN

October 31st

O LORD God of hosts, who is mighty as you are, O LORD, with your faithfulness all around you? Psalm 89:8.

Over the years, Halloween has become one of the most troublesome holidays for Christians to celebrate. Once considered a children's holiday, a modern rise in paganism has made some Christians wary of celebrating it in any way.

We get the name from "All Hallow's Eve" or the evening before All Saint's Day. Despite this, most Halloween customs have a pagan origin. Most people consider Halloween Druidic in origin, with additional customs blended into the observance from Roman tradition.

The Celtic tribes considered November 1 to be New Year's Day. When the Romans conquered Britain and began introducing their customs, three celebrations fell on the same day: festivities for the Roman sun god, the goddess Pomona, and Samhain (pronounced Sow'en). Most of the traditions remained Celtic, but sacrifices, such as horses, to the sun god, became a part of the day. Sometimes celebrants burned men, usually criminals, in wicker cages.

People celebrated Cernunnos, the Celtic god of the underworld at Samhain. Artists often depicted Cernunnos with antlers, leading Christians to associate him with Satan. In Celtic tradition he was not associated with evil in the sense that Satan is. In addition to being the god of the underworld, he was the god of plenty.

The Celts believed that during the New Year's celebrations, the dead came back to join the living. On Samhain Cernunnos judged the souls and decided their fate. He sent sinful souls into the bodies of animals for the next twelve months. Those found worthy were still dead, but allowed to remain in human form. People could sway his favor through gifts and sacrifice.

Roman worship of Pomona also shaped the festivities. She was the goddess of orchards and the harvest. The festival in her honor featured apples, nuts, grapes and other fruits. These parts of the celebration have come down to today in the form of apple bobbing and, until recently, using nuts to tell fortunes at Halloween.

People still sacrificed horses at Samhain as late as A.D. 400. Gradually, the church assimilated this sacrifice with oxen substituted for horses. Pope Gregory I, who had charged English missionaries to keep as many local customs as possible, issued this statement about the practice: "They are no longer to sacrifice beasts to the Devil, but they may kill them for food to the praise of God, and give thanks to the giver of all gifts for His bounty."

Though we have no definite proof, this decree seems to begin the process of blending Samhain and Christian tradition. The process continued when, in the eighth century, Pope Gregory III moved the church festival of All Hallows to November 1st. On that date he dedicated a chapel in Rome in honor of All Saints. In the next century, Pope Gregory IV decreed it a universal church observance.

By the Middle Ages, people believed witches and sorcerers favored the eve of All Saint's Day. A witchcraft cult devoted to Satan worship grew up around Halloween. Part of the cult included periodic meetings or witches' Sabbaths, with the most important on All Hallow's Eve. On that night Satan supposedly mocked the feast of the saints with unholy rites. The idea of witches flying on broomsticks grew out of this time period.

The roots of modern Halloween parties go back to this time, as well. To avoid facing evil alone, people gathered together and told of strange or spooky experiences to pass the time. They played traditional games such as bobbing for apples. Refreshments might include apples or nuts from the new crop just harvested.

Since the spirits were closer at Halloween, and the spirits supposedly knew about the affairs of men, people used various divination methods and accepted the results seriously. Pranks and mischief were also common. The perpetrators often dressed in masks and wore clothing of the opposite sex. The "spirits" received credit for the results of any mischief.

Many of the customs flourished in Ireland, Scotland, Wales, and parts of England well into the eighteenth century, and some into the nineteenth. A common survivor was lighting bonfires to disperse the spirits. Farmers would set up pitchforks plaited with straw and set them on fire to singe the witches' brooms if they came too close.

American observance of Halloween came fairly late, as most early settlers were Protestant. They left saints' days behind them along with any folk customs attached to them. Only a few scattered and regional observances of Halloween took place. That changed with the Irish potato famine and resultant wave of immigration in the 1840s. Most of the immigrants were Catholic, bringing with them both the religious observances and the folklore remnants of Samhain.

Halloween had become a national observance in the United States by the late 1800s. The Victorian fascination with entertainment of various kinds, coupled with a rise of anti-Catholic feeling, led to a reinvention of the holiday. Halloween became a time for adult parties, not children's gatherings.

Like many earlier harvest related parties, Halloween gatherings often served to allow courting between young people. Divination games became popular, especially to predict future mates. The first haunted houses appeared at Victorian era Halloween parties, when hosts and hostesses converted basements into chilly, spooky caverns.

Costumes appeared for the first time at late Victorian parties. Magazines of the time period detailed suggestions for successful parties and gave ideas for invitations, decorations, and activities.

By the beginning of the twentieth century, a new realism began to take over the previous preoccupation with entertainment and the supernatural. Magazines began focusing on more intellectual matters such as travel, history, politics, and current events. As the times changed, so did the celebration of Halloween.

New books focused on the fun elements of Halloween for children. Party books gave instructions on entertainments appropriate for children, avoiding elements that might be too frightening. Games similar to those used at today's Halloween carnivals today began appearing, and scavenger hunts and musical chairs replaced matchmaking.

The custom of Mischief Night survived the changes, and most people were tolerant of innocent pranks. As time passed, though, Mischief Night became more than harmless fun. Vandalism began occurring under the guise of mischief. To prevent these problems on Halloween, groups began holding parties to keep children occupied, beginning in 1908. In the 1920s Anoka, Minnesota organized the first citywide supervised party to keep young revelers out of trouble.

Different cities tried a variety of ways to reduce vandalism. Citywide parties were a popular and successful method. So were various clubs encouraging the children themselves to look out for potential vandals. With the onset of World War II, cities cracked down further on vandalism. What had once been a nuisance became a threat to national security.

After the war, Halloween had become a children's holiday again. Though vandalism was still an occasional problem, much of the mischief association with Halloween had diminished. As communities grew, citywide parties became impractical. The focus switched to the classroom and the home. School classes celebrated Halloween and mothers planned in-home parties for their children.

Trick-or-treating developed as a nearly universal custom during the 1950s. Part of the idea came from the former citywide parties. Children had become used to trading good behavior, i.e. no vandalism, for candy and treats at parties. Trick-or-treating was an outgrowth of that idea.

Halloween has begun to swing back to the adults again. Adult parties with participants in full costume are now popular. This time, though, it's not just for adults. Children still have their share of the celebration.

While much of modern Halloween focuses on entertainment, modern day pagans consider it a time of celebration. Various neo-pagan groups celebrate both Beltane and Samhain as the two great festivals of the year. For Samhain, observances include communion with one's dead ancestors and perhaps leaving out food and wine as offerings to the dead.

Halloween Symbols and Customs

Costumes

Wearing costumes on Halloween has a variety of possible explanations. You may be able to go back to the pagan New Year's feast, where villagers greeted ghosts with a banquet. At the end of the feast, people wore masks and costumes representing the souls of the dead and paraded to the outskirts of town, leading the ghosts away. The first Christian rationale for the earlier custom was groups of costumed children who offered to fast for departed souls in return for money or a food offering.

Another explanation is that costumes may stem from the practice of displaying saints' relics on All Hallows. In poor churches that couldn't afford relics, some parishioners dressed as patron saints, with the remainder of the congregation as angels or devils. Even this change may well have come from old memories of dressing as the dead to lure ghosts away.

More recent costumes have reflected modern culture. In the 1920s children's costumes reflected the various images and interests of the decade: Charlie Chaplin, cowboys, Indians, and clowns. By the 1950s, the media began to play a role in costume selection. Little girls began dressing as princesses, brides, and angels, while boys might be army men or hoboes. Through the years since then, each popular movie, television show, or toy line begets a multitude of miniature replicas each Halloween.

The familiar black and orange colors of Halloween come from the different parts of its development. Black is a traditional color representing death, while orange comes from the color of ripening fruit like pumpkins.

Trick-or-treating

Trick-or-treating is likewise obscure. We can see the most similarities to an ancient Irish practice on Halloween when groups of peasants went from house to house asking for money to buy delicacies for a feast. The groups requested contributions in the name of Muck Olla, a Druid deity or St. Columba, the monk who led the conversion of Scotland and founded a monastery on Iona off the Scottish coast. They promised prosperity to the generous and threatened the stingy.

In America, trick-or-treating began to become popular between 1920 and 1950. It began in the wealthier parts of the East and spread from there throughout the West and South. Reports noted trick-or-treating in Wellesley, MA in the late 1920s, but it was the 1940s before it had spread to North Carolina, Florida and Texas.

Trick-or-treating for UNICEF (The United Nations Children's Fund) is a recent innovation. In 1950 children from a Sunday school near Philadelphia sent in $17.00 they had collected trick-or-treating. The idea caught on and expanded. A presidential proclamation on October 27, 1967 making October 31st National UNICEF Day in the United States, made the connection official.

The Jack-o-Lantern

The Jack-o-Lantern, while familiar today as a symbol of Halloween, does not seem to have the same background as the other symbols. Although Celtic in origin, it does not seem to be connected with the celebration of Samhain.

We can find several variations of Jack's story. All of them involve him having tricked the Devil in some way. One story says that he tricked the Devil into climbing an apple tree to get an apple. Then, he cut a cross into the tree to keep him from climbing back down. Once he had the Devil trapped, Jack made him promise he would never come for Jack's soul or claim it in any way.

When Jack died, heaven rejected him, but when he tried to enter hell, the Devil turned him away, as he had promised never to take Jack's soul. Both heaven and hell were closed to him, leaving Jack stranded and doomed to wander the earth eternally.

As a parting gift, the Devil threw Jack a coal from the fires of hell to light his way. Jack had been eating a turnip, so he put the coal inside. Ever since, he has traveled the earth with his lantern. Over time, people used other vegetables besides turnips, including rutabagas, potatoes, and the now familiar pumpkin.

NOVEMBER

Born in November happy is she,

whom the topaz teaches fidelity.

Birthstone: Topaz

Birthstone Virtue: Fidelity and Friendship

Flower: Chrysanthemum

November is another of the "number named" months, taking its name from the Latin *novem* or nine.

ALL SAINTS DAY

November 1

"Then they will deliver you up to tribulation and put you to death, and you will be hated by all nations for my name's sake. Matthew 24:9.

As early as the fourth century, people suggested a special day be set aside to commemorate all the martyrs. Some had suffered martyrdom in groups or for other reasons no one knew their names. Practicality played another role in the suggestion. The year was not long enough to have a separate day for each martyr.

Eastern churches have observed various dates since the fourth century. St. John Chrysostom preached a sermon every year to venerate all the saints. The day began in the Roman church when Pope Boniface IV consecrated the Pantheon in Rome in A.D. 609. Formerly the temple of the old Roman gods, he consecrated it to the Virgin Mary and all the martyrs. Yearly observances began in May 610.

Pope Gregory III changed the date from May to November and enlarged it to include all saints, not just martyrs during the consecration of the chapel at St. Peter's Basilica in Rome. Though some say he intended this change to Christianize or overshadow the lingering remnants of Samhain, other scholars argue that the change was for more practical reasons. Celebrating on November 1st made foods from the fall harvest available to feed the many pilgrims coming to Rome for the feast.

In the 830s Pope Gregory IV established the feast in the church calendar as All Saints' Day. He required all Catholics to observe it, including the vigil of preparation on All Hallow's Eve.

THANKSGIVING

Date varies - 4th Thursday in November

Sing to the LORD with thanksgiving; make melody to our God on the lyre! Psalm 147:7.

Setting aside a day to offer thanks goes back to Greek festivals for Demeter or Roman ones for Ceres. Anglo-Saxons celebrated a "harvest home" with a feast. In Scotland a *kirn* included special church services and a large dinner. For Jews, the eight-day Feast of Tabernacles provides an opportunity to offer God thanks.

The first American settlers knew about thanksgiving from both Christian and non-Christian traditions, but the first thanksgivings in America were strongly Christian based. So when did the very first Thanksgiving happen in America? The answer depends on your definition of "thanksgiving."

Modern Americans think of thanksgiving in terms of the holiday feast. For the original Pilgrims, a thanksgiving was one of three allowable holy days: the Sabbath, the Day of Humiliation and Fasting, and the Day of Thanksgiving and Praise. They also celebrated successful harvests, but in their minds a harvest celebration and a thanksgiving were two different events.

If we take thanksgiving simply as thanking God, colonists who founded the short-lived Popham Colony at what is now Phippsburg, Maine held the first American celebration August 9, 1607. After their two ships reached one of the Georges Islands off the Maine coast, the Rev. Richard Seymour led the group in "gyvinge God thanks for our happy metinge & saffe aryval into the country."

Then next contender for "first Thanksgiving" came on December 4, 1619. Colonists at Berkeley Hundred – a plantation settlement near Jamestown – dedicated a day to give thanks for their company's survival. The settlers continued to observe the day until 1622 when a conflict with the Native peoples nearly devastated the colony.

The generally accepted first thanksgiving took place at Plymouth Colony in 1621. Though they didn't record a date, they must have held the celebration between September 21, when the shallop returned from Massachusetts Bay, and November 9th, when the Fortune arrived with new settlers. They probably considered this a harvest celebration. A day of Thanksgiving might end with a feast, but would not include games and other recreations as reported for this first celebration. Their first official Thanksgiving holy day took place in 1623 after rain saved the colony's crops.

Nationally, the Continental Congress declared the first Thanksgiving in 1777. We can see a clear distinction between a harvest celebration and a day of thanksgiving. The proclamation specifically said that "servile labor and such recreations as, though at other times, innocent, may be unbecoming the purpose of this appointment, be omitted on so solemn an occasion." Over the following years, government declared various other Thanksgivings until the custom fell out of use after 1815.

President Lincoln re-established the tradition in 1863 when he declared two Thanksgivings, one on Thursday, August 6th, and the other for the last Thursday in November. Eventually, Lincoln's choice of the last Thursday in November became the traditional celebration date. Congress passed legislation in 1941 making the fourth Thursday of November a national holiday.

Some scholars suggest that the Feast of St. Martin of Tours, or Martinmas, may have inspired some of the original customs. During medieval times, the feast was an almost universal harvest and thanksgiving celebration held on November 11. The festive meal featured roasted goose. Celebrants drank St. Martin's wine – the first made from newly harvested grapes. However, the Puritans did not celebrate saint's days. If Martinmas contributed customs, they came from another group.

Our celebrations today are a combination of the more solemn holy day and harvest festivals. Even football games and other sports played on Thanksgiving have their roots in the shooting contests and other games from the first Thanksgiving.

The First Thanksgiving - a closer look

So what did the first Thanksgiving itself look like? Did the Pilgrims eat turkey and dressing with cranberry sauce? We only have two accounts of the first Thanksgiving and neither gives many specifics of the meal itself.

Edward Winslow recorded in his diary, "Our harvest being gotten in, our governor sent four men on fowling, that so we might after a special manner rejoice together after we had gathered the fruit of our labors." The four men killed enough fowl, of an unspecified variety, to feed the company for a week.

During the celebration, they apparently had some type of games or sports, though they only mention practicing with their guns. The Native peoples also came and joined the feast. Their leader, Massaoit, brought ninety men with him.

Winslow records that the Natives stayed for three days, and that they went out and killed five deer, which they brought back to the settlement. Some sources speculated that they didn't have enough food with the additional people. Perhaps they were aware that their presence at the feast had strained the colonists' resources.

Winslow ends by stating, "And although it be not always so plentiful as it was at this time with us, yet by the goodness of God, we are so far from want that we often wish you partakers of our plenty."

William Bradford's *Of Plimouth Plantation* reports on the harvest season preceding the first Thanksgiving. "They began now to gather in the small harvest they had, and to fit up their houses and dwelling against winter, being all well recovered in health and strength and had all things in good plenty." He mentions a variety of different activities the colonists carried out to prepare for winter. They did a good bit of fishing, storing many of the fish for the winter, and also began gathering waterfowl.

Bradford mentions the colonists taking many wild turkeys and deer. They also had meal, with corn added from the crops they had grown the first year.

From these two sources, we know that fowl of some sort was available, along with fish and venison. They may have had wheat as well as the corn. Beyond that, we can only speculate from knowing what was probably available to them.

We can more easily say what they didn't have. Most likely, they had no beef, pork, or chicken. Records for the Mayflower do not indicate that the colonists took any animals with them, other than two dogs. Some think they probably brought animals, even if records don't mention them. Even if they did, the colonists probably wouldn't have slaughtered any for food, as they were attempting to build up their stock. Eggs and goat's milk may have been available.

Apples and pears would not have been part of the meal. Those trees aren't New England natives, and the new trees they planted would take years to bear fruit. They knew about potatoes and sweet potatoes, but these vegetables weren't present in early New England.

Both the Pilgrims and the Native peoples grew a flint variety of corn, which isn't good as corn-on-the-cob or popcorn. They may have parched the corn, which will make it puff up slightly, but not pop like true popcorn. Even though they had corn, "Indian pudding" would not have been present as we know it because they did not have molasses.

They might have used native cranberries in some types of puddings or stuffing, but not in the familiar jelly on our tables. The colonists didn't have sugar to make it. They'd never heard of celery, and they used bread crumbs or egg yolks instead of flour to thicken sauces or gravy.

Undoubtedly, they offered a prayer of thanksgiving just as we do now. Today, we often call this a table grace. The word comes from the Latin *gratiae* or "thanks."

Thanksgiving Symbols

The Turkey

The familiar Thanksgiving turkey may have been present at the first feast. Bradford does mention taking turkeys in the hunt. Since other meat and fish are also mentioned, the turkey probably wasn't the centerpiece of the meal as it is today. The word turkey for our American bird came with the Pilgrims. In England turkey meant a guinea fowl. Traders imported this bird from Turkey and eventually it acquired the country's name. When the colonists saw the similarity to the American bird, they gave it the same name.

The Pilgrims

Every year in November, the familiar black and white dressed pilgrims begin to appear in stores. Those first settlers would be surprised and bewildered to see their modern appearance, beginning with buckles on hats and shoes. People did use buckles as decorations, but not until later in the seventeenth century, after the time the Pilgrims settled Plymouth.

Artists have exaggerated the large collars and cuffs in our modern conception of Pilgrim dress. The women's aprons would be larger than those usually shown on the "typical" Pilgrim. Nor did all of the settlers wear black, except on Sundays and special occasions, since they associated black with dignity and formality. Their celebration was a special occasion, but not a formal one. For every day wear they dressed in the colors and fashions that others of similar station wore.

One of the biggest changes, though, would be in the name itself. The name Pilgrim didn't become common until the mid-nineteenth century. The Pilgrims called themselves "Separatists" or "Puritans" when speaking of their faith. They called each other saints, and the other colonists who made up their group, strangers.

Indians

Most Thanksgiving pictures include the Native people living in Massachusetts when the Puritans first arrived. Many pictures show them with the feathered bonnets of the Plains tribes. The Massachusetts Wampanoag people had a tribal culture quite different from the Plains Indians. Though they did use animal skins for clothing, they didn't wear feathered bonnets.

A teepee is out of place in a Thanksgiving picture, too. The Wampanoag built conical wigwams or *weetos* from cattails. The *weetos* varied in size, with larger ones for families that could house up to fifty people.

Cornucopia

Next to the turkey and the pilgrims, the cornucopia or "horn of plenty" is one of the best-known symbols of Thanksgiving. Unlike the other symbols, it has its roots in Greek and Roman mythology. According to some sources, the horn of plenty was an attribute of Flora and Fortuna, both Roman goddesses. The cornucopia represented the unending gifts the gods gave mortals and artists pictured it with fruit and other gifts flowing freely from it.

In other sources, the cornucopia belonged to the Greek goddess Amalthea, a nymph who took the form of a goat to nurse the infant Zeus in a cave on the island of Crete. In this story the horn was always full of whatever food or drink someone wanted.

The term cornucopia is from the Latin *cornu copiae*, which simply means "horn of plenty," the other commonly used name.

DECEMBER

December's child shall live to bless

the turquoise that insures success.

Birthstone: Turquoise, Zircon

Birthstone Virtue: Great success and happiness, prosperity in love

Flower: Narcissus

The last of the months named for numbers, our twelfth month comes from the Latin *decem* or ten.

HANUKKAH

Date varies - November/December

The LORD is my light and my salvation; whom shall I fear?
The LORD is the stronghold of my life; of whom shall I be
afraid? Psalm 27:1.

Since Hanukkah is close to Christmas, many Christians know the name. Hanukkah is actually an extra-Biblical holy day, at least for those who do not recognize the Apocrypha as part of Scripture. The main sources for the story behind Hanukkah are the deuterocanonical books, First and Second Maccabees, and the writings of Josephus, making it the most historically documented Jewish holiday.

The story behind Hanukkah takes place between the two Testaments. In the fourth century B.C. Alexander the Great conquered Israel along with the remainder of the Near East. After his death, Israel fell under the domination of the Seleucid dynasty. Finally, in 167 B.C., Antiochus Epiphanes decided to force everyone under his rule to accept Greek culture.

He outlawed all Jewish rituals and replaced temple worship with the worship of Greek gods. While some Jews did bow to pressure, others resisted and died as martyrs. The turning point came when a group of Greeks came to the village of Modin and set up an altar. They commanded the Jews to sacrifice a pig to show they had accepted the Greek religion.

When an old priest, Mattathias, saw a Jew about to do so, he became angry and spoke to the crowd:

"Even if all the nations that live under the rule of the king obey him and have chosen to do his commandments, departing each one from the religion of his fathers, yet I and my sons and my brothers will live by the covenant of our fathers. We will not obey the king's words by turning aside from our religion, to the right hand or to the left." I Maccabees 2:19-22.

After this declaration he killed the man preparing to make the sacrifice. He and his five sons fought the Greeks, fled to the mountains, and began a guerrilla war. Before dying, Mattathias turned leadership over to his son Judah the Maccabee. Eventually, he and his followers retook Jerusalem and reclaimed the temple.

The Greeks had defiled temple, and Judah could find only one small container of oil to light the temple menorah. The container had only enough oil for one day, but the menorah burned for eight days. The celebration of Hanukkah focuses on the Maccabees' successful fight for independence and the miracle of the oil.

Some sources leave out the miracle of the oil entirely. Perhaps the differing accounts depend on the focus of those telling the story. Despite the historical difficulties, Hanukkah remained a popular – though minor – festival.

The proximity to Christmas has influenced the celebration of Hanukkah, especially here in America. The tradition of giving children Hanukkah money is an old one, but gift giving has become a part of the holiday. Some give a small gift each of the eight nights of Hanukkah, while others choose to give only one larger gift.

The modern celebration of Hanukkah focuses on lighting the menorah. Participants light one candle each night after sunset, adding a candle each night until all eight burn on the eighth night. Oil is traditional for Hanukkah lights, but most people today use candles.

Games are another Hanukkah tradition, particularly the dreidel or top. Dreidels have a different Hebrew letter inscribed on each of the four sides: *nun, gimel, heh, shin*. These are the first letters of the phrase *neis gadol hayah sham* or "A great miracle happened there." Modern Israelis replace the letter shin with *peh* for the word *poh*, to make it read "A great miracle happened here."

You can play a variety of different games with the dreidel. One game involves trying to spin the dreidel upside down or seeing how many one person can spin at once. Trying to knock down other spinning dreidels is another favorite.

Rabbis permit games of chance during Hanukkah, so one popular game has players put a stake in the pot to start the game. People don't necessarily use money, though some include coins. They may also wager nuts or other items. Players then take turns spinning the dreidel. The letter facing up when the dreidel falls over decides the game. If *nun* lands up, the player neither wins nor loses. Spinning *heh* wins the player half the pot, while *gimel* wins the whole pot. A *shin*, on the other hand, requires the player to contribute one coin or other item.

Because of the miracle of the oil, eating foods fried in oil is also customary. Traditional foods include potato latkes or *sufgainiyot*, a type of doughnut.

ADVENT

Date varies - November/December

A voice cries: "In the wilderness prepare the way of the LORD; make straight in the desert a highway for our God. Isaiah 40:3.

Many Christians think of Advent as the four Sundays preceding Christmas. Others may think of it as the days from December 1st to December 24th, thanks to Advent calendars. For those in liturgical churches, Advent begins the church year, with the first Sunday of Advent always the one nearest the feast of St. Andrew the Apostle on November 30.

The earliest record of a time set aside to prepare for Christmas is a decree Bishop Perpetuus of Tours issued in A.D. 490. He required a fast held three days of every week from the Feast of St. Martin (November 11) to Christmas. At that time, people called this *Quadragesima Santi Martini* or the 40 Days' Fast of St. Martin's.

Over the years, the practice spread, though Rome adopted it slowly. In the sixth century Roman Christians began to celebrate Advent, but as a time of joyful celebration rather than one of penitence. During the reign of Pope Gregory the Great in the sixth century, the four-week time period had become common. By the ninth century the celebration was fairly universal in both Eastern and Western churches, though the length of time could still vary.

The two traditions – penitential and joyful preparation – remained separate for some time until an accident of history helped them join

121

into one season. Some churches in the Frankish territory of Gaul (the area including modern day France) had begun to use liturgical books from Rome. Then Pope Stephen crowned Pepin, the predecessor of Charlemagne. To honor the occasion, the new king commanded people to use the Roman liturgy throughout his kingdom.

Scribes had to hand copy the books and send them out, leaving time for the two Advent themes to mix. When Charlemagne assumed the throne, he continued the effort. However, he authorized his advisor to write substitute portions for pieces missing from his books. The result was a true blend of the two traditions.

The blend might not have become widespread except for a decline in the Roman church during the tenth century. When the Roman emperors ordered a reform at the end of the century, they borrowed liturgical books from the north. What they received was the adapted liturgy. No one realized the change, so they considered the blended liturgy authentically Roman. The mixture of joy and penitence became the liturgy for the whole medieval Roman church.

We get the word Advent from the Latin *adentus*, meaning coming or arrival. An old tradition says that the four weeks of advent represent the four comings of Christ: as a man, in a human heart, at the individual believer's death, and in the future at the Last Day.

Advent Symbols

Advent Wreath

As with so many customs, we have Germany to thank for the Advent wreath. Pre-Christian customs associated with Yule celebrations, especially fires and lights, may be similar to using candles in the Advent wreath, but the modern custom is much more recent. Using lights as a symbol of Advent only dates to the sixteenth century. As fitting for Christmas preparation, the symbolism reminds people of the Old Testament when humanity remained in darkness waiting for the coming of Christ.

Wreaths are an ancient symbol of victory and glory. Using a wreath to prepare for Christmas points to the coming of Christ and the glory of His birth. The wreath can also point to the unending love of God. The evergreens used in the wreath are a reminder of the eternal life Jesus came to give.

Advent Candles

The four candles placed on the wreath may vary in color. People use all purple or all blue, or a mixture of three purple and one pink. Purple is the liturgical color of penitence, so purple is appropriate to the season. The pink candle symbolizes rejoicing and belongs on the Third Sunday of Advent. Some churches call this Gaudete Sunday from the first word of that Sunday's Latin mass: *Gaudete* or Rejoice. Using two candle colors illustrates the mixture of penitence and joy in Advent.

The candles don't have fixed meanings. Different churches may assign different meanings for each Sunday. Some may focus on themes such as love, peace, and joy. Others may look at characters from the Nativity story. One common set of themes for the Sundays are:

First Candle: The coming of Jesus - both His birth and His eventual second coming
Second Candle: Continue to focus on the coming of Jesus
Third Candle: John the Baptist, the herald of Christ
Fourth Candle: Mary, God's obedient servant

Some people also add a fifth candle to the center of the wreath as the Christ Candle. This candle is usually white, the traditional color of purity. Those who use five candles light one each of the four Sundays preceding Christmas, and light the Christ Candle on Christmas Eve or Christmas Day.

The colors of the candles aren't as important as the symbolism of the flame: Christ coming as a light in the darkness. Using the traditional colors can add meaning, but the key is to remain focused on preparing to celebrate Jesus' birth.

SAINT NICHOLAS'

DAY

December 6

Blessed is the one who considers the poor! In the day of trouble the LORD delivers him; Psalm 41:1

We have little historical information about Nicholas despite the fact that he is well known today. He was born around A.D.280 in Patera to wealthy Christian parents. He became bishop of Myra at thirty years of age and earned a reputation as a protector of the innocent.

Emperor Diocletian had him imprisoned for his faith, but Emperor Constantine later freed him. People also knew Nicholas as a defender of the faith. He was present at the Council of Nicaea, where clerics argued about whether Christ was divine or merely human. He argued passionately for Christ's divinity.

Some sources say Nicholas died on December 6th, 343, while others say he died around 350, possibly on December 6. His grieving parishioners buried him in Myra. His body remained in Myra until 1082 when people removed it and took it to Bari, Italy, where it remains buried to this day.

As with many saints, legends grew up around his life. One of the most common stories, with several variations, tells of him giving money to a local merchant who was about to be forced to sell his oldest daughter into slavery or prostitution. To prevent this, Nicholas threw a small bag containing enough money to provide a dowry through the window. When a similar fate threatened the next two daughters, he again gave money to provide for their marriage.

One variation of the story has the money landing in a stocking hanging on the hearth to dry. Later this part of the story would lead children to hang their stockings by the chimney for Santa Claus to fill.

In the twelfth century, French nuns began distributing candy to children on St. Nicholas Day. Gradually children believed St. Nicholas himself left the gifts if they had been good. Bad children received switches to frighten them into good behavior.

By the Middle Ages, St. Nicholas had become the most popular of all the saints. He had more churches named for him during this time than all the apostles together. We also see the first blurring of St. Nicholas' life with other ideas. The German myth of the god Odin became associated with St. Nicholas. In older belief, Odin flew over villages by night to see if villagers were caring for their crops and stock as they should.

After judgment became part of St. Nicholas' legend, a person dressed as St. Nicholas visited children's homes and asked questions about Scripture and the catechism, and whether they had been good or bad during the year. Black Peter accompanied him and wrote down the names of children who didn't know the right answers or who had been naughty. St. Nicholas then encouraged them to do better before Christmas.

When the Protestant Reformation began, St. Nicholas was among the first traditions the new church dropped. Martin Luther knew it would be hard to give up old customs like St. Nicholas, so he made a change in the custom. Instead of a saint, the gift giver became the *Christkindl* or Christ child. As an added touch, Jesus came on His own birthday, instead of St. Nicholas' day. In America, the German *Christkindl* became Kris Kringle.

St. Nicholas came to America with Dutch immigrants. They also brought their term for him: *Sinter Klaas*, which people Anglicized as Santa Claus. This Santa Claus was still very much a bishop. He wore the bishop's red and white robes and miter. Rather than the fat jolly man of today, he was still slender and often shown with his hand held up in blessing.

Santa Claus now overshadows the earlier St. Nicholas, a circumstance that would sadden him, but not because he wanted glory for himself. As a man of God, St. Nicholas would want people to remember Jesus at Christmas.

CHRISTMAS

December 25th

And she gave birth to her firstborn son and wrapped him in swaddling cloths and laid him in a manger, because there was no place for them in the inn. Luke 2:7.

During the Roman Empire, people usually celebrated the birthdays of rulers and other outstanding people, though not necessarily on the exact date of their birth. The early Christians' desire to honor Christ's birth may have come from the fact that they gave Him the title and other honors that pagans paid to the "divine" emperors. These Christians lived in a culture where the birth of a ruler was a major celebration. What could be more natural than celebrating the birth of the King of Kings?

Despite the logic of this, controversy has long surrounded Christmas. In A.D. 245 Origen wrote that it was sinful even to consider observing Jesus' birthday "as though He were a King Pharaoh." Early Christians in Armenia and Syria accused Roman Christians of sun worship for celebrating Christmas on December twenty-fifth.

When Oliver Cromwell took command during England's Commonwealth years, he banned Christmas celebrations and required citizens to go about their business as usual. When the Puritans settled America, they brought their distrust of Christmas with them, so people didn't celebrate Christmas at Plymouth. William Bradford reported in his diary, "ye 25th day begane to erect ye first house for comone use to receive them and their goods." The following year, 1621, the governor again insisted that work continue as usual.

A group of new settlers had joined the original group, and when Governor Bradford discovered a group of them on Christmas:

"at play, openly: some pitching the barr and some at stoole-ball, and shuch like sports. So he went to them. . .and tould them that it was against his conscience, that they should play and others worke."

Even Governor Bradford could be reasonable. He told them that if keeping Christmas was a matter of devotion for them, then they could stay in their homes to remember the day. He would not, however, allow any kind of the games or other celebrations commonly part of an English Christmas at that time. According to the account, after his rebuke, no one made another open attempt to celebrate Christmas.

In 1659, Massachusetts made observance of Christmas a penal offense:

"Whosoever shall be found observing any such day as Christmas and the like, either by forbearing labor, feasting, or any other way upon such account as aforesaid, every such person so offending shall pay for each offense five shillings as a fine to the country."

Despite this decree, reportedly a few people celebrated in Massachusetts. The government finally repealed the law after much argument in 1681. King Charles II had requested its repeal earlier and they agreed lest their hesitation seemed to detract from the king's authority.

Though the settlers gave in to the King in the matter of banning Christmas, the status of the holiday was still unsettled. In 1686 the newly appointed Governor Andros had to hold Christmas services in the Boston Town Hall rather than the Puritan meeting house.

Even though the Puritans dismissed Christmas, we have early records of Christmas celebrations in the New World if not directly in America. On December 25, 1492, Columbus' ship the *Santa Maria* caught on a reef off the coast of Haiti and wrecked. They built a fortress from the ship's timber which they named *La Navidad* or nativity.

French settlers on St. Croix Island off the coast of Maine held a service in 1604. Settlers in Jamestown, Virginia, held the first clearly recorded American celebration in 1607. Forty of the one hundred original settlers commemorated the day in their wooden chapel. They experienced so many difficulties that winter that they were more inclined to be thankful for survival than indulge in a lavish celebration.

In 1613, Captain John Smith's diary gives us a look at his expedition's celebration of the holiday:

"The extreame wine, rayne, froast and snow caused us to keepe Christmas among the salvages where we were never more merry, nor fed on more plenty of good Oysters, Fish, Flesh, Wilde fowl and good bread, nor never had better fires in England."

Shortly after American independence, Elizabeth Drinker, a Quaker herself, divided Philadelphia into three categories on how Quakers dealt with Christmas. The first were Quakers who "make no more account of it than another day." The second group celebrated the day as a religious observance while the third "spend it in riot and dissipation." In those three groups she neatly summed up the way different groups viewed Christmas over the years.

As people settled the Southern states, Christmas came with them. Many gentlemen farmers fostered Christmas as both a sacred time and a time for relaxation. They kept many Old World traditions alive, including caroling, the Yule log, and decorative greenery. They added others such as fried oysters, eggnog, and a Christmas morning fox hunt.

In the South, Christmas became a time for a full house and a full larder. Thanks to the warmer Southern temperature, Christmas came not long after harvest season, so a holiday break for rest and enjoyment seemed natural. The season was a time to meet friends and family, and sometimes for weddings.

French settlers in Louisiana introduced firecrackers as a part of Christmas celebrations. The custom spread to other areas throughout the South, varied with shooting guns instead. Hearing fireworks at Christmas is still common today in the South.

Christmas and the Sunday Schools

Considering the fact Christians still debate various Christmas customs, it is interesting that during the first half of the nineteenth century in America, Sunday Schools helped promote the acceptance of folk customs such as the Christmas tree and Santa Claus. While they didn't deliberately do so, that was the end result of a curious division of thought about Christmas as a holy day and as a holiday.

Just as with the denominations that sponsored them, Sunday Schools varied on whether they accepted Christmas as a holy day. Methodists tended to disapprove, as did Presbyterians and Baptists. The Episcopal, Catholic, and Lutheran churches accepted Christmas as part of their heritage.

For churches that didn't believe Scripture sanctioned Christmas, literature for December did not include the Nativity. Because cultural customs like the Christmas tree and Santa Claus fell outside the liturgical cycle and church year, they didn't see the customs as in conflict with church aims. Sunday Schools adopted what they saw as a pleasant and enjoyable celebration for children.

In 1846 the Advocate, a Philadelphia Methodist Sunday School publication, ventured to wish boys and girls a happy Christmas. They carefully included caution not to have "a merry, foolish one devoted to mirth and trifling and mingled with sin." The first Sunday School Christmas tree may have been at the Episcopal Church of the Holy Communion in New York City in 1847. Under the leadership of Dr. William A. Muhlenberg,

"The wealthier parishioners provided the gifts for their less well favored little brothers and sisters, all the poorer children of the church, and in unloading the heavy boughs and distributing the fruit to the eager, expectant hands, feasted themselves on the blessedness of giving as better than receiving."

The celebration also included singing carols and a time of fellowship.

A wave of German immigration that peaked between 1850 and 1854 spurred acceptance. Methodist churches, in particular, responded to the new immigrants by supporting German mission school programs. The Germans, in return, brought their own customs with them and tenaciously held onto their own holiday celebrations. People didn't see their customs as associated with any particular ecclesiastical persuasion and adopted them.

By1859 Christmas trees were a frequent but not universal feature of Christmas in New York Episcopal Sunday Schools. The custom spread along with Western expansion. By the late 1860s Santa Claus began appearing at Iowa church suppers.

Rev. S. Hermann, who was a missionary among the Plains Indians reported on his Christmas from Omaha, Nebraska in 1865.

"We had a Christmas festival at Bellevue and one at Fort Calhoun. The one at the latter point was the first in the history of that town. About sixty dollars were spent to decorate the tree, and procure presents for the Sunday-school;"

He goes on to tell of the books he got from the Church Book Society, and mentions the great interest in Christmas activities, considering that they had held the first services only six months previously. The parish at Bellevue raised about the same amount of money for their festival.

Iowa had a community tree in Franklin County in 1868. At the time, three different denominations held services in the second floor courtroom of the Hampton courthouse. All three denominations joined in planning the tree.

Finding a tree presented a problem to the group, as evergreens are not common on the Iowa plains. Someone remembered that cedar trees grew along the river, so Rev. L. N. Call and a deacon traveled 20 miles to cut one. Volunteers then decorated the tree with candles and popcorn garlands, along with apples for color. They hung some presents on the lower branches with the rest at the base.

Their service followed a pattern similar to many across America. They began by singing, followed by a Scripture reading, and then a prayer. Afterwards, people distributed presents and the recipients opened them. A special committee provided a sack of candy for each child, while parents and Sunday School teachers brought other gifts. Though mainly for children, the needy and elderly also received gifts. A farewell address followed and a child recited the already well known "'Twas the Night before Christmas."

The custom still took time to spread. In 1872 none of the children in North Madison, Iowa had seen a tree, so the Sunday School planned one for them. Prudently, they planned a church party and a play in case they couldn't locate an evergreen. The townsman who finally provided a tree charged $1.00 for it, but he had earned it. As he crossed the river to cut the tree, the ice broke and he fell in. Finally they brought in the ten foot tall tree and decorated it with popcorn and candles.

In her semi-autobiographical book *On the Banks of Plum Creek*, Laura Ingalls Wilder tells of the first Christmas tree she had ever seen. The events in the book took place in about 1875. Obviously, the tree still hadn't penetrated all areas since Laura didn't even recognize what it was when she first saw it.

The tree in *On the Banks of Plum Creek* illustrates another facet of the spread of Christmas customs. Many churches in the settled areas sent donations of clothing and toys to frontier areas where pioneers were struggling to settle new land. The gifts Laura and her family received came from just such a collection.

Along with clothing and toys, churches sent out their church papers as well. The publications included details of Christmas celebrations their churches held, including Christmas trees, Santa Claus visits, and other entertainments. The frontier churches then followed the lead of their city counterparts.

In stark contrast to the many voices raised in protest of Christmas and Christmas celebrations, one man worked to have other Protestant denominations accept them about the same time Christmas trees were spreading in Sunday Schools. Rev. Henry Harbaugh, a Reformed churchman had spent eighteen years writing and preaching to promote Christmas. In 1867 he wrote of his dismay at the attitude shown by the Scotch-Irish community near Harrisburg where he was living.

"Here where I am living - in the westerning Pennsylvania hills - they want to hear nothing of Christmas. They spend the day working as on any other day. Their children grow up knowing nothing of brightly lit Christmas trees, nor Christmas presents. God have mercy on these Presbyterians - these pagans."

Despite Rev. Harbaugh's frustration, by the end of the nineteenth century, most churches accepted Christmas. They had adopted the folk customs, and gradually they accepted the day as a holy day. The denominational literature showed a gradual change to allowing at least one December lesson to focus on the Nativity.

Once churches accepted Christmas as Jesus' birthday, either actual or commemorated, concerns began growing about the surrounding customs. At the beginning of the twentieth century many churches accepted the Sunday School Christmas tree and Santa Claus without comment. Other churches began rejecting them for fear they encouraged greed and crowded Christ out of Christmas.

In response churches began to change their approach. In 1914 Phebe Curtiss wrote a Christmas service called White Gifts for the King. As part of the program, children brought white wrapped gifts for the needy. The real change, though, was that they presented them as birthday gifts for Jesus. The idea spread rapidly and White Christmas became common in Sunday Schools.

With the beginning of World War I, focus on the needy changed to the needs of refugees overseas. This grew into a general missions emphasis. Christmas programs focused on specific groups needing help, and often featured costumed children representing Japan, Korea, or other nations.

Based on a survey of churches done in 1927, Santa Claus began losing favor in church Sunday Schools while programs focused on worship and drama became more popular. People didn't ask if they should celebrate Christmas at church. The question became how to do so without losing the major focus of Christmas: Jesus' birth.

As we enter the twenty-first century, the question still remains. Christmas today is the biggest holiday of the year, but Christians still wonder how, or if, it should be celebrated. Both Sunday Schools and individuals struggle with how to handle the variety of customs and traditions built around the celebration of Jesus' birth.

Christmas - the year and the date

A.D. 1?

We're used to thinking of our calendar as based on anno Domini, "the year of our Lord," so learning that Jesus wasn't born the first year A.D. can come as a shock. When Dionysius Exiguus reformed the calendar, he dated the Nativity in the year 753 from the founding of Rome, the customary method used at the time. His date was correct for the founding of Rome, but not for the birth of Christ. Changes in the calendar since his first reformation moved Christ's birth from the first year A.D.

Since Herod the Great died in 4 B.C., and he is a major part of the Nativity story, Jesus must have been born some time before the date of his death in 4 B.C. Some scholars estimate Jesus' birth at 5-4 B.C., while others suggest it was as far back as 8-7 B.C. The Christian lawyer Tertullian, writing in A.D. 200 when Roman records were still accessible, said that the birth of Jesus occurred 7 or 8 years before the supposed date.

Other attempts to pinpoint the exact date center on Luke's statement that the census taking Mary and Joseph to Bethlehem occurred "while Quirinius was governor of Syria." The problem is that records show Quirinius did not become governor of Syria until A.D. 6-7. Though some use this to accuse Luke of inaccuracy, an archeological inscription indicates that Quirinius may have served an earlier term as governor.

Census records available from the Roman Empire show that they took censuses at fourteen year intervals, with records available from A.D. 20, 34, and 48. Counting back from these dates, the Empire should have conducted censuses in 6 A.D. and 8 B.C. The latter date is possible for Jesus' birth, though somewhat on the older end. Another option is that the census mentioned in Luke may have been a provincial one rather than one of the larger censuses covering the entire empire.

December 25th

Through the years, people have suggested a variety of different dates for Jesus' birth. Early Christian theologians in Egypt set the date as May twentieth. Other churchmen chose late March or April, close to Passover. Others chose January 1, coinciding with the New Year on the Roman calendar.

Scripture itself gives only a few clues. Shepherds were in the fields watching their flocks by night. This suggests that the birth took place during the spring lambing season, as winter nights can drop below freezing, and shepherds would have their flocks in a sheepfold.

Others point out that you can see sheep in the fields year round in the Middle East. The fat-tailed breed of sheep common in Israel is hardy and able to be outside year round. While the occasional night may be cold, on many nights shepherds and sheep would be in the fields.

Over the years, the dates most frequently put forth were March 25, December 25, and January 6, which became Epiphany. The church may have chosen December 25 for practical reasons, since it coincides with winter solstice. Former pagan celebrations held on December 25 include Mesopotamian celebrations for Marduk, Greek ones for Zeus, and Roman Saturnalia in honor of Saturn.

If this was the case, persecution may have played a role in the selection. When your faith carried a death penalty, blending in with your surroundings was sensible. By celebrating something different on the same date, Christians appeared to be taking part in "approved" religion, thereby protecting themselves from persecution.

Or, much like today's idea of friendship evangelism, early Christians may have looked at same day celebrations as a way of sharing their faith with their pagan neighbors. By adopting similar traditions, but giving them a Christian meaning, they could share their faith in a way that would make it approachable to others.

Another possibility for choosing December 25 as Jesus' birthday stems from the fact that the church at this time believed that Jesus had died on March 25. To people at that time the mystery of the Incarnation included both Jesus' conception and His death. They got this idea from the Jewish tradition of identifying the birth and death of patriarchs on the same day, in this case birth being conception. Nine months after March 25th is December 25th.

Others looked at the creation of the world to give a date for the Nativity. They believed God created the world on March 25 - the spring equinox. Since day and night are equal then, they must have been equal when God divided darkness from light. God's division would be perfect. Surely Mary conceived Jesus on the same day God created the world. Again, December 25 is nine months from March 25, assuming that Jesus' gestation would also be perfect to the day from His conception.

In *De Pascha Computus*, an Italian or African writing from A.D. 243, the author used the same logic about the date of the world's creation, but decided on March 28th as Jesus' birthdate. The author reasoned that God made the sun and moon on the fourth day of creation. The Sun of Righteousness, then, would be born on the same day. The light of the physical and spiritual worlds would correspond.

St. John Chrysostom, writing in A.D. 386, says that Julian (Pope Julius I A.D. 337-352) made an extensive investigation of the correct birthday of Christ. He found that the Western churches celebrated on December 25, while the Eastern churches recognized January 6. In the end, after taking all arguments into account, Julian chose December 25th in 350 A.D.

The date spread quickly. Gregory of Nazianzus introduced December 25 as the Nativity in Constantinople in 379. Gregory of Nyssa reported it in Cappadocia in 380. St. John Chrysostom established it in Antioch in 386. Alexandria accepted the date in 431 and Jerusalem shortly thereafter.

Once people accepted the date, many began looking for ways to prove that December 25 was the historically accurate date of Jesus' birth. They made a number of assumptions based on the gospel accounts of the Nativity. First, they assumed that Zechariah was serving in the Holy of Holies on the Day of Atonement, which would be around September 25. Therefore, his son John would have been born on June 24. Working from John's conception and the information the angel gave Mary at the Annunciation, Mary conceived Jesus on March 25 and gave birth to Him on December 25.

In the Roman world, December 25 was *Natalis Solis Invicti*, the Birthday of the Unconquerable Sun, during which people honored the sun god, Mithras. Originally a Persian deity, Mithras was extremely popular in Rome, and this celebration gradually blended with Saturnalia.

Despite the similarity of the date, Christians were very aware of the differences between their celebration and those of the Romans. St. Chrysostom wrote,

"They called this December 25, the Birthday of the Invincible One (Mithras); but who was so invincible as the Lord? They call it the Birthday of the Solar Disk; but Christ is the Son of Righteousness."

Church leaders rebuked new converts who kept using external symbols of sun worship.

In A.D. 274 Aurelian proclaimed Mithraism the Roman Empire's official state religion. For many years, it vied with Christianity as the most popular religion in the Roman Empire, a sound reason for wanting to prevent confusion between the two. In fact, many parts of Mithraism and Christianity were quite similar. The competition between the two ended when Constantine declared Christianity to be the official religion of the Roman Empire in A.D. 313 and Mithraism slowly died out. With the date officially set and Christianity spreading, today's familiar customs began gathering around Christmas.

The word *christmas* dates from around 1050 when people called the feast "Christes Maesse" or "Christ's Mass." The familiar merry in our

Merry Christmas had a somewhat different meaning originally. People once used *merry* to mean "blessed, peaceful, or pleasant" rather than "joyful or happy" as it does now. In combination with mass as in a church service, "Merry Christmas" pointed to spiritual blessings more than to a wish for a happy holiday.

The First Christmas - a closer look

When St. Francis created his first manger scene, he helped continue the process of adding elements to people's understanding of Jesus' birth. When we think of Christmas, we have an image drawn from popular representations and songs. Unfortunately, Scripture and history don't support many of our preconceived notions of the first Christmas.

Most people see Jesus' birth happening in a wooden stable open at the front. A wooden hay-filled manger stands in the center. Animals stand to the side or in the background. Jesus lies in the manger with Mary kneeling nearby and Joseph standing on the other side. Shepherds and their sheep approach, and the three wise men ride up on their camels. Over the entire scene shines a large star.

This makes a pretty picture, but is it accurate? As with the date, Scripture gives very few details. We can glean more from what people have learned of life in Jesus' day. Let's take a closer look at what the first Christmas really may have looked like. Please bear in mind that this "debunking" of the myth isn't intended to take away any of the wonder of Christ coming to earth. If anything, a more realistic picture makes it even more amazing that God chose to come to us in such a way.

The Stable and the Manger

Scripture tells us that Jesus lay in a manger. From this, many have assumed over the years that He must, therefore, have been born in a stable. People also adopted the European idea of a stable. We have two possibilities for Jesus' place of birth.

From Scripture, we know the inn at Bethlehem had no room, so Mary and Joseph may well have taken shelter in the inn's stable. At the time when Christ was born, a stable was not a separate wooden building, but a cave. The area near Bethlehem is home to many caves used to house livestock.

The Church of the Nativity in Bethlehem, built over the traditional site of Jesus' birth, stands over one of these caves. On entering the cave, we find a manger in the spot where tradition says Mary laid Jesus. Rather than the wooden kind we think of today, it is stone, carved from the rock of the cave, as was common at the time.

The second possibility is that a family in the town took in Mary and Joseph. Since Joseph came from Bethlehem he should have had relatives there. In many of the poorer homes, the stable was a lower portion of the house itself. You entered into the family's living quarters and took a step down into the animals' area. In an already crowded home, this might be the only place available to offer shelter to the young family, and the manger still made a convenient place to lay a new child.

Whichever version is correct, the traditional wooden stable and manger probably bear no resemblance to Jesus' actual birthplace. More likely, it was either a cave or the stable end of a family's mud brick home.

Does the Church of the Nativity stand over the place where Jesus was born? Judging the authenticity of most sites in Israel is nearly impossible. Centuries of wars and occupations brought many changes. However, the Church of the Nativity has a history that goes back nearly to the time of Christ.

Writing about A.D. 160, St. Justin wrote "Joseph lodged in a certain cave near the village; and then, while they were yet there, Mary gave birth to the Christ and placed Him in a manger." During this time, the Roman Empire was persecuting Christians and soldiers deliberately desecrated Christian holy places by putting pagan shrines over them.

They treated site of the current Church of the Nativity like others, dedicating a shrine to Adonis, and planting a grove in his honor. However, this had the effect of marking the site rather than obscuring it. Several early church writings indicate that people knew the location over time. Origen, for example, stated that even the pagans knew where Jesus was born and would point it out to pilgrims.

Later, St. Jerome wrote, "In the cave which had heard the tender wailings of the infant Christ, the lover of Venus was bemoaned." This verifies both the fact that people knew the cave as Jesus' birthplace and pagan worship took place there later.

After the Emperor Constantine converted to Christianity, he ordered a basilica built over the cave. A Samaritan revolt in 521-528 almost ruined the building, but the Emperor Justinian had it restored in 565.

A few years later, in 614, the Persians invaded Israel and destroyed Christian shrines in Nazareth and Jerusalem. They spared the basilica in Bethlehem by a curious chance. According to contemporary stories, a mosaic on the church showed the wise men as Persian magi. When the invaders recognized their dress as that of countrymen, they were afraid to harm the church.

All of this provides a strong case for the Church of the Nativity marking the actual birthplace of Christ, and many accept it as authentic.

Swaddling Clothes

Many modern nativity sets show Jesus with His arms stretched wide, as if reaching out to the world. While this is a nice symbolic gesture, it would have been impossible in reality. To wrap a child in swaddling clothes, the mother folded a square of cloth around the baby's body with the child's arms inside the cloth, too.

Once she had wrapped the child, she held the main cloth in place with wide bands of cloth four or five inches wide and five to six yards long. The band also went under the chin and across the forehead. The bands' appearance could vary. Poor woman might use nothing more than strips of cloth while more well-to-do mothers embroidered their bands.

Shepherds

The Bible mentions shepherds and sheep regularly. From the Patriarchs to King David and his Shepherd's Psalm it's hard to imagine the Bible without sheep or their shepherds. Particularly during the Old Testament period, Israel was a land of shepherds.

During the time when nearly every family had a few sheep, the task of shepherding them fell to the youngest son. The older sons in the family were learning a trade and their time was too valuable to spend in the fields all day. If the family didn't have sons, or if the family only owned one or two sheep, a village shepherd took all the sheep out to pasture.

A shepherd had few tools. He carried his scrip: a bag made of skins to hold his meal and a few stones for his sling. The rod in the 23rd Psalm was a club he carried for protection. Made of oak, the rod had a knob at one end, and shepherds frequently drove nails into the knob for extra defense.

The staff served as a walking stick, while the shepherd used the crook in the end to pull a sheep gently back into line. Another of David's tools, the sling, was quite simple: merely a leather pouch with a strip of sinew or rope on either side. Despite its apparent simplicity, the sling was an effective weapon. Stores in modern Bethlehem no longer sell slings because of the danger they pose in skilled hands.

In addition to the necessities, most shepherds carried a double flute made of reeds. These provided entertainment for the shepherd and soothed the sheep. The Arabic word equivalent to psalm in Hebrew, *mazmoor*, means "played on a pipe or flute."

In America, we think of shepherds driving their sheep. In Israel and other parts of the Middle East, shepherds did and still do lead their sheep. The sheep know their shepherd and his voice, and follow along behind him.

A shepherd's job was difficult. Not only did they have to watch over their flocks night and day, they had to protect them from wild animals. They cared for the sheep during lambing time, sheared them, and made sure they had enough to eat and drink.

At night, the shepherd brought his flock within a sheepfold - a large, open, stone-walled pen. In a permanent sheepfold, shepherds might build a low shelter along one wall to provide extra protection for the flock. As the sheep entered the fold, the shepherd held his rod over the door and counted each one. The shepherd then slept at the door of the fold to be sure nothing could get in to harm them.

Often shepherds put several flocks together at night. The individual shepherds shared the task of watching over the flock. The next morning the shepherds easily divided their flocks. Each shepherd simply called his sheep to him.

There's certainly no doubt that the shepherds were present at the Nativity, since Luke's Gospel records that they went at once to find the child. The interesting thing about the shepherds is that they *were* present. While people once regarded caring for flocks as a good occupation, shepherds had become the outcasts of Jewish society. Being out in the fields for extended periods of time made it difficult for them to maintain ritual purity or attend services at the synagogue regularly. Courts would not allow shepherds to testify.

Some speculate that the shepherds mentioned in Luke were not general shepherds but those in charge of watching over the flocks raised for sacrifice at the temple. If this is true, it adds poignancy to their presence at Jesus' birth. The ones who raised the sacrificial lambs came to see the Lamb who would make the final sacrifice.

The Wise Men

Who were these "wise men" who visited Jesus? How many of them were there and where did they come from? What were their names? The answers may surprise you.

While we frequently refer to them simply as "wise men," the word Scripture uses for them is *magi* which comes from the Old Persian *magu*, referring to a hereditary class of priest-scholars. However, neighboring Eastern countries used the term as well, making it difficult to pinpoint their land of origin. They were probably astronomers, astrologers, or both. While they studied the stars as an astronomer would, they also believed that the movements of the stars foretold events on the earth.

Two major groups of magi existed: Persian and Babylonian. We don't know which group Matthew meant. The name comes from Persia, and early Christian tradition gives them Persian names and shows them in Persian garments. On the other hand, the Magi may have been Babylonians, since astronomy reached its highest development in Mesopotamia, and the star plays a major role in their visit.

We also don't know how many came. The traditional number of three comes from the three gifts – gold, frankincense, and myrrh – listed in Matthew. People assumed that each individual brought a different gift. Another legend said that the wise men represented all humanity as the three races descended from Ham, Shem, and Japheth, the sons of Noah. This legend also explains why artists show one of the Magi as a black man.

Some believe that because of the difficulty and danger of travel, an entire caravan traveled together to follow the star, making thirty or more magi possible. Other theories suggested anywhere from two to twelve. Both St. Augustine and St. Chrysostom gave the number of magi as twelve.

Scripture doesn't mention how they traveled. Some saw their mounts as representing the three known continents. The horse came from Europe, the camel from Asia, and the elephant from Africa.

The magi don't become kings until the sixth century. The Venerable Bede provides a list of the names and descriptions of each man in his book *Collectanea et Flores*.

The king tradition came from prophecies describing the conversion of pagans, though now scholars don't believe they were meant to refer to the wise men. Isaiah 60:3-6 says, "And nations shall come to your light, and kings to the brightness of your rising. Lift up your eyes all around, and see; they all gather together, they come to you; your sons shall come from afar, and your daughters shall be carried on the hip. Then you shall see and be radiant; your heart shall thrill and exult, because the abundance of the sea shall be turned to you, the wealth of the nations shall come to you. A multitude of camels shall cover you, the young camels of Midian and Ephah; all those from Sheba shall come. They shall bring gold and frankincense, and shall bring good news, the praises of the LORD."

The magi had well established names by ninth century. People knew them as Caspar (Gaspar or Jaspar), king of Tarsus; Melchior, king of Arabia; and Balthasar, king of Saba (Ethiopia) or Sheba. They also had other names. The Greeks referred to them as Appellios, Damaskos, and Amerios, while in Hebrew they were Galagat, Sarachin, and Malagat.

Artists began picturing them with crowns and in regal attire sometime after the eleventh century. Other legends grew up around them. People believed they knew each king's origin along with their ages and specific descriptions of their gifts as well. Melchior was sixty years old and brought gold in a casket shaped like a shrine. Artist showed Gaspar as a beardless youth of twenty. His gift was myrrh in a gold-mounted horn. Balthasar, traditionally a black man, was forty years old. He carried frankincense in a jar shaped like a censer.

While gold is well known, the other gifts are not as familiar. Frankincense is *olibanum*, a gum resin often burned as incense, and once used as medicine. People ground the small whitish beads or chunks into powder before they burned them, producing a scent similar to balsam. The tree that frankincense comes from grows among bare rocks in the mountains of southern Asia and northeastern Africa.

Myrrh is also a resin, orange-colored, from trees of the *Commiphora* family. It was expensive, and used for perfumes, anointing oil, medicine, and embalming.

As time passed, people attached symbolism to the gifts. The gold represented royalty, given to a king; the frankincense, divinity, or perhaps was for a high priest; and the myrrh, death, since people used it to prepare bodies for burial. Contrarily, some thought myrrh was for the great physician. While these associations make sense, other scholars believe the Magi chose these items simply because they were valuable and easy to carry.

Another part of the legend says that the wise men received gifts in return for those they brought. In return for the gold, they received charity and spiritual wealth. For the frankincense, perfect faith, and for the myrrh, perfect truth and meekness.

Some stories say that they made their journey in twelve days, during which they did not need to rest, eat, or drink, as it seemed like only a day to them. Then, after they returned to their own countries, they gave away all their possessions to the poor and traveled sharing the good news of the birth of Jesus, the Prince of Peace. Eventually, they traveled to India, where they met St. Thomas, who baptized them and ordained them as priests. There they died as martyrs for their faith.

The line between truth and fiction blurs three hundred years later, when the Empress Helena, mother of Constantine the Great, had their supposed bodies taken to Constantinople. Later, following the first crusade, people moved the bodies to Milan. When Emperor Barbarossa conquered Milan in 1164 he gave the relics to Raynaldus, Archbishop of Cologne. He had the bodies moved there, where people now call them the Three Kings of Cologne.

The Star

What about the star the Magi followed? Turning to Scripture again, we have little detail. According to Matthew 2:1-12, the star went ahead of the Wise Men until it stopped over the house where Jesus lay. Since people in biblical times didn't make distinctions among objects in the sky, this leaves us without being certain as to whether or not that was what we today would call a star. The Greek word used in Matthew, *aster*, can mean any luminous heavenly body.

People approach the star of Bethlehem in one of three ways: with a supernatural viewpoint, a rational viewpoint, or a historical viewpoint.

The supernaturalist looks at the account as literal history and the star as a supernatural event created solely to herald Jesus' birth. We don't need to try to explain the star, just accept it. Also, since God created the star solely for the birth, it fulfilled its purpose and no longer exists.

The rationalist considers the entire story to be a myth with symbolic, rather than literal, meaning. He or she might suggest that the star was part of another god's story which tradition transferred into the Nativity account.

The historical approach considers the story to be true, and looks at the star as a way to test its truth in the context of history. They look for astronomical evidence to support the star, much as Biblical archaeologists look for physical evidence to support events told in Scripture.

Those looking at the star from the third viewpoint have come up with a variety of different possibilities to explain the star of Bethlehem. While each of these does look for a natural explanation, finding one doesn't take away from the story. God timed the natural event specifically to mark Jesus' birth.

The first possibility is that the star was a large meteor. This would create a spectacular sight in the night sky, but meteors do not last for more than a few seconds. They also are local, rather than visible to a large area. In addition, the impact from the meteor would have left a crater as further evidence. Because of this, most scholars do not believe that the star could have been a meteor.

A more likely possibility, assuming a natural explanation, is a comet. Comets move slowly and are often visible for days. They may be bright enough for people to see in the daytime. Further, a comet can appear to "stand" over a location, and the tail can point at a particular location, both of which fit Matthew's record. Chinese records show a comet visible in 4 B.C. from February to April, providing a likely candidate. Modern astronomers list a comet that would have been seen a year previously in 5 B.C., giving another possibility.

Yet another candidate is a new star or a nova. Though these are not as conspicuous as comets or meteors, a nova is still a possibility. Historians credit Hipparchus with recording a new star in 134 B.C. Though this star comes at the wrong time to have been the actual star of Bethlehem, the record shows that people of that time were sufficiently familiar with the skies to recognize a new star's appearance.

People have identified the nova Tycho Brahe discovered in 1572 as the star of Bethlehem more than any other astronomical object. He worked out a periodicity for it which made it a logical possibility. The

Chinese also observed a nova in 4 B.C.

The last possibility is a conjunction of planets. Remember that the term star could mean anything seen in the sky, and that the Magi were astronomers. In fact, the Magi believed the planets were gods, and their movements could foretell events. Under their belief system, Jupiter was the king of the gods and Saturn the protector of the Jews. They saw the constellation of Pisces as the House of the Hebrews.

Archaeologists found a contemporary reference on ancient records of the School of Astrology at Sippar in Babylon. Written in cuneiform, the inscription refers to three conjunctions. In 7 B.C. records show conjunctions of Jupiter and Saturn on May 27, October 5, and December 1. Three conjunctions in one year were unusual. Since the Magi knew the Jews were expecting their Messiah, added to the fact that the conjunctions took place in Pisces, the conjunctions could have led them in search of the Messiah.

As logical as this theory seems, we still have a problem with these conjunctions. They would not come to stop over the house where the child lay. Nor would they move in the way we usually think of an object traveling through the sky to a specific place. Some suggest that "following" the star referred to the meaning the Magi got from the conjunctions.

Another intriguing possibility is that the star was several of these possibilities. First, the conjunctions of Jupiter and Saturn in 7-6 B.C. alerted the Magi to what was happening in Israel. Then, the comet of 5 B.C. reinforced an important happening, and sent them on their way. Finally, the comet of 4 B.C. appeared after they reached Jerusalem and asked Herod for further information, guiding them the last step.

Christmas Symbols and Customs

Candy Canes

Recently, the legend of the candy cane has become quite popular but the legend is just that: a legend. No one candy maker created the candy cane. For the symbolism, here is the traditional story of the candy cane.

A candy maker designed the candy cane to tell the Christmas story. He began with white candy as a reminder of Jesus' purity, but he also made it hard, for Jesus is our Rock. He added peppermint flavor for the gifts of spices the wise men brought. When he curved one end, the cane became a crook - a reminder of the shepherds who were the first to hear of the newborn King and of He who is the Good Shepherd. Turned upside down, the cane is a J for Jesus - the name given Him to remind us "He will save his people from their sins." The red stripes remind us that He was born to die for us. As the Scripture says, "By His stripes we are healed." When you see candy canes this Christmas, think of more than a decoration. Remember the true meaning of Christmas: the gift of our Savior, Jesus Christ.

The candy cane does provide a reminder of the shepherd's crooks. One source said that St. Nicholas' bishop's crook became Santa Claus' candy cane. The shepherd and bishop's crook are related. The bishop's staff reminds him that he is the shepherd of his flock, just as Christ is the Good Shepherd. We usually see the candy cane as a reminder of the shepherds at the nativity, but it can also refer to a Pastoral shepherd.

The candy cane got its start many years ago when a choirmaster in Cologne, Germany handed out sticks of hard sugar candy to restless youngsters at a living Nativity in the Cathedral. In honor of the occasion, he had the candy maker bend the sticks into a shepherd's crook. The tradition spread and candy canes, often decorated with red roses, became traditional gifts accompanying Nativity plays.

The tradition came to America with German settlers. In 1847 an immigrant in Wooster, Ohio named August Imgard decorated a small spruce with paper ornaments and candy canes. The first candy canes were white, not striped. Christmas cards before 1900 show plain white canes, but an 1834 lithograph shows what appears to be a red and white striped candy cane.

In the lithograph, a family is returning from Christmas shopping. One child carries a long red and white striped cane with a crook, including a second bend like a bishop's or shepherd's crook. Nothing in the picture tells us if this is a candy stick, but the only other possibility would seem to be a toy shepherd's or bishop's crook. This is possible, but the stripes seem odd on a toy of that type.

In another of her books, *Little House on the Prairie*, Laura Ingalls Wilder describes receiving red and white striped peppermint candy sticks in their Christmas stockings. She calls them "long, long sticks of candy," not candy canes. We know this had to be before 1874, when the Ingalls had moved to Walnut Grove, the time she describes in On the Banks of Plum Creek. Assuming she remembered correctly, not thinking about later candy canes, this would put both red stripes and peppermint flavoring together earlier than sometime after the turn of the twentieth century as another source stated.

People used both wintergreen and peppermint in early striped canes, but eventually peppermint became the most common flavoring. Peppermint fits well symbolically, since it is akin to hyssop, which represents healing. People also used hyssop to place the blood on the doorpost of homes at Passover. Some say that the peppermint reminds us of the Wise Men and the spices they brought. Times do change. In sixteenth century England, people thought of mince pies as symbols of the Wise Men because of the spices used in them.

In the 1920s Bob McCormack began making candy canes as a special Christmas treat for children, friends, and local shopkeepers in Albany, Georgia. He made his canes by hand, which required a lot of time to twist, cut, and bend each one individually. This limited him to local production.

Bob's brother-in-law, Gregory Keller, a Catholic priest, invented a machine to automate the production of candy canes in the 1950s. This allowed the company to produce larger numbers easily. When they also came up with new ways to package the completed candy canes, they could ship nationwide and the candy cane became a familiar part of Christmas everywhere. Today Bob's Candies is still the largest producer of candy canes in the world.

Father Keller frequently told people to remember the symbols involved when they saw a candy cane. He, too, saw the white background as representing purity, while the red was the color of blood, a symbol of sacrifice. The wide red stripe symbolized Christ's sacrifice while the smaller red stripes stood for the sacrifices His followers make for the Kingdom.

Chrismons

Chrismons are a new addition to Christmas traditions. The first Chrismon tree appeared in the nave of Ascension Lutheran Church in Danville, Virginia in 1957. The idea for the tree came from a desire to make the traditional Christmas tree – which many considered out of place in a church – more meaningful for Christians. The word *chrismon* comes from a combination of the words **Chris**t and **Mon**ogram.

A Chrismon, then, is an ornament that is a monogram for Christ. Over time, people applied the term to other symbols, not just initials, but all point directly to Jesus. You can use a variety of different materials, but all should be a combination of gold and white. White is the liturgical color for Christmas and stands for the Lord's purity and perfection. Gold traditionally represents majesty and glory. White lights on the tree carry out the theme and also point to Jesus as Light of the world.

Church symbols offer a rich variety of possibilities for a Chrismon tree. Enough different cross designs exist to fill an entire tree without even researching other possibilities. A good book on church symbols will provide many more options. Teachers often use Chrismons in children's departments to help underscore the true meaning of Christmas.

Christmas Candles

Some speculate that part of the imagery of Jesus as Light of the World, especially lighting candles or fires, may go back to the connection with sun worship. People of lowers station considered candles an appropriate gift to those of higher station during *Natalis Solis Invicti*. According to R. T. Hampson writing in England in 1841, this idea was still around at that time.

"The poor were wont to present the rich with wax tapers, and yule candles are still in the north of Scotland given by merchants to their customers. At one time children at the village schools in Lancashire were required to bring each a mould candle before the parting or separation for the Christmas holidays."

In Scandinavia, a large candle burned as a companion to the Yule log from Christmas Eve to Twelfth night, representing the divine light that had come into the world. In Norway, people lit two candles on the table every evening until New Year's Day.

Confusion over candles seems to have begun fairly early. St. Jerome told Vigilantius that they used candles in church express Christian joy, not to expel darkness.

Others give the tradition of lighting Christmas candles a later date and don't connect them with remnants of paganism. One source stated that the modern custom of lighting Christmas candles came from Ireland. Legend states that they were to guide Mary and Joseph to a home where they would be welcome. A more practical explanation is that they arose during Catholic suppression to show priests homes where it was safe to enter and say mass.

Christmas Cards

Several different items pre-dated our current Christmas cards. English schoolboys made "Christmas pieces" for their parents. The boys wrote verses or greetings for their parents on paper with colored borders and headings. These showed parents their son's progress with their handwriting. Occasionally adults also used more elaborate sheets for verses or messages to send with a gift or letter, though they were not common.

Early wall calendars carried seasonal wishes. Other forerunners included the visiting card or calling card, illustrated note paper, and birthday greetings. All of these helped promote the later growth of Christmas cards by developing printing methods and mass production techniques.

One contender for the first Christmas card is a card designed by a sixteen year old London artist named William Egley. The British Museum displays this card as part of its collection. The controversy comes from the blurred date. We aren't sure if the card comes from 1842 or 1849.

Most sources recognize the card J.C. Horsley created for Sir Henry Cole in 1843 as the first. Sir Henry found that he was too busy to write a large number of Christmas letters to his friends, and requested the card as an easier way to keep up his correspondence. Horsley, a member of the Royal Academy, suggested printing extra copies of the card and offering them for sale. The resulting lithographed card was hand-colored, though presumably not by the busy Sir Henry.

This first card was less than a success. Sir Henry Cole sent approximately 300 copies, and a few sold commercially, but the new idea met with a mixed reaction. Though some liked the novel idea of an illustrated card, the scene of a family celebrating with wine glasses in hand offended members of the temperance movement.

Cards gradually became more popular in the 1860s, when members of the Royal Family began to commission artists for special holiday paintings. They had the paintings reproduced in color on Christmas cards. Later in the decade, London's Marcus Ward and Company began using artists to design Christmas cards, including Kate Greenaway who later became famous as a children's book illustrator. By 1870 England had accepted the Christmas card as part of the seasonal customs.

In America, the Christmas card developed a little later, though handwritten cards were common by the time of Andrew Jackson. In fact, people sent so many that the superintendent of mails in Washington, D.C. formally complained to Congress around 1882, asking that they pass laws to prohibit exchanging cards by mail. The extra Christmas mail had forced him to hire additional workers. His petition was not well received.

Perhaps this was the same official who complained to the Washington Star:

"I thought last year would be the end of the Christmas Card mania, but I don't think so now. Why four years ago a Christmas Card was a rare thing. The public then got the mania and the business seems to be getting larger every year. I don't know what we will do if it keeps on."

We know Louis Prang as the father of the American Christmas card. He was a German exile following the German revolution of 1848. In 1875 he perfected a process of lithographic color printing using 8-12 plates, and began making Christmas cards shortly thereafter. The first cards had mainly floral designs such as apple blossoms, roses, daises, and geraniums. Later he introduced more typical Christmas scenes, both secular and sacred.

Prang's cards were larger than those we often think of today, and the high quality printing he used made them frameable art pieces. Many people gave them instead of a small gift. He also began using classic artworks on his cards in an attempt to share them more broadly.

Prang held to high quality standards for his cards. He refused to make tasteless comic cards or trick mechanical ones. Even his humorous cards were more artistic caricatures than exploiting crude humor.

In 1880 he sponsored an open competition for Christmas card designs with a first prize of $1000, and several lower prizes. He used the competitions to obtain the best art for his cards, but he also wanted to educate public tastes and stimulate an interest in original decorative art among art students.

His time as the leader of the industry was short. Around 1890, merchants began importing lower quality and less expensive cards. Prang's cards, selling for $1.00 apiece, were costly for the time. Rather than lower his quality to lower price, he stopped producing cards. Today, collectors highly prize his cards.

When he left the card industry, he began focusing on other projects. In addition to his other achievements, Prang introduced the idea of providing art instruction to public schools as the Prang Method of Education. He also worked with producing art supplies.

Christmas Trees

Using trees as part of religious celebrations goes back well beyond the first recorded Christmas tree. Egyptians erected green date palms indoors for winter solstice rites. Romans hung trinkets on pine trees during Saturnalia and used evergreens as part of *Natalis Solis Invicti*. In Britain, Druids placed candles, cakes, and gilded apples in tree branches as offerings.

Like many other customs, church leaders initially opposed using a tree to celebrate Christmas. Tertullian, the Christian lawyer, wrote clearly about the difference between Christian and pagan in terms of Christmas customs.

"Let them (the pagan) kindle lamps, they who have no light let them fix on the doorposts laurels which shall afterwards be burn, they for whom fire is close at hand. . . . But thou (Christian) art a light of the world and a tree that is ever green; if thou hast renounced temples, make not a temple of thy own housedoor."

In 575 Bishop Martin of Bracae forbade the use of all greenery and "other dangerous Calend customs." Christians didn't accept trees as decorations for Christian homes until the sixteenth century, though they used other greenery earlier.

So how did trees become associated with Christmas? Hundreds of years separate trees used for the Christian celebration of Jesus' birth from older pagan customs. We can only be certain of one thing: they are German in origin. However, we have three different stories of how evergreen trees became part of the Christian celebration of Christmas.

The earliest points to Boniface, an eighth century English missionary we know as the Apostle of Germany. The details vary. All the stories say that Boniface cut down an oak tree sacred to Odin, where pagans had offered sacrifices. When he did so, some stories say a young fir tree miraculously sprang from the stump of the oak. Others say he found the fir growing at the roots of the oak, while other versions say he brought the fir and set it up on the stump of the oak.

Regardless of how the fir came to be there, the stories agree that he removed the sacred oak and replaced it with a fir tree. Legend records him speaking to those around him:

"This little tree, a young child of the forest, shall be your holy tree to-night. It is the wood of peace, for your houses are built of the fir. It is the sign of endless life, for its leaves are ever green. See how it points upward to heaven. Let this be called the tree of the Christ-child; gather about it, not in the wild wood, but in your own homes; there it will shelter no deed of blood, but loving gifts and rites of kindness."

The remaining two stories came later. During the fifteenth century in Germany and other parts of Europe, mystery plays became popular. These were religious plays designed to help those who could not read learn Bible stories. In the medieval church December 24 was Adam-and-Eve's Day. One of the props used was a fir tree hung with apples. This paradise tree represented the Garden of Eden's tree of the knowledge of good and evil.

The church placed the two days next to each other deliberately. Celebrating Adam and Eve just before Christmas brought out some Christmas theology. The first Adam fell, but Jesus was the second Adam who repaired the fall of the first Adam.

Later, the church suppressed the mystery plays. People had added new characters and ideas, obscuring the Biblical message. The Paradise tree then found its way into individual homes. The timing of the day coupled with imagery of Jesus as the Tree of Life may have helped the evergreen regain a place in holiday celebrations.

As time passed, people added white wafers to the tree, representing the bread used in communion. This paired apples representing the fall of man with symbols of the Body of Christ, the Redeemer of fallen man. In time, these led to cookies cut in a variety of shapes. As late as 1952, people in some sections of Bavaria, still called small trees decorated with lights, apples, and tinsel *Paradeis*, echoing the paradise tree.

Probably the most familiar tale of all is the story of the Reformer, Martin Luther, walking home one winter evening. As he looked up, the stars in the sky seen through the branches of the evergreen trees reminded him of the Star that shone over Jesus' birthplace. The evergreens drew him to think of the everlasting life Christ came to offer.

When he arrived at home, he cut down a small evergreen and brought it into his home. He put candles on the branches as a reminder of the stars and of Jesus as light of the world. Others later adopted and expanded the custom and the Christmas tree was born.

People today consider the story legendary, but adds a nice touch to the season. Perhaps the story has some root in fact, since Martin Luther loved the Christmas season and celebrating the Savior's birth. He may have helped popularize and spread the custom of decorated trees.

Candles weren't originally part of the tree. People displayed candles on a separate decorated pyramid representing Christ as the Light of the World. However, as the tree gained popularity, the candles and other decorations moved from the pyramid to the tree sometime in the mid-seventeenth century.

The first Christmas trees were small enough to fit on a table with a crèche. Gradually, people began to use larger trees and the crèche went under the tree instead. The star displayed over the crèche moved to the top of the tree. Perhaps the alternate favor tree-topper, an angel, can trace its roots to the same source.

The earliest recorded account of a Christmas tree is from 1605. "At Christmas time in Strassburg they set up fir trees in the rooms, and they hang on them roses cut of many-colored paper, apples, wafers, gilt, sugar. . . ." By the 1700's the custom was firmly imbedded in Germany.

Despite the widespread nature of the custom, the controversy did not die out. Writing in the 1740s, Rev. Johann Konrad Dannhauer of Strassburg said,

"Among other trifles with which the people often occupy the Christmas time more than with God's word, is also the Christmas or fir tree, which they erect in the house, and hang with dolls and sugar and thereupon shake and cause to lose its bloom. Where the habit comes from, I know not. It is a bit of child's play. . . Far better were it for the children to be dedicated to the spiritual cedar tree, Jesus Christ."

At first, Christmas trees were mainly a German custom. Hessian troops introduced them to America during the Revolutionary War, but they did not gain a widespread acceptance. When German settlers came to Pennsylvania in the early nineteenth century, they brought the Christmas tree with them.

The first mention of a Christmas tree in America comes from the December 20, 1821 diary entry of Matthew Zahm of Lancaster, Pennsylvania. In 1830, we have the first known exhibition of a Christmas tree, with tickets sold for 6 1/2 cents each. People must have considered Christmas trees exotic and unusual for someone to sell tickets to view one. President Franklin Pierce set up the first Christmas tree inside the White House in 1856. By 1877, the custom was well established. A writer for the Weekly Press of Philadelphia stated, "As well might we dance without music, or attempt to write a poem without rhythm, as to keep Christmas without a Christmas tree." Later, in 1923, President and Mrs. Calvin Coolidge began the custom of lighting the National Christmas tree on the White House grounds.

In England, Prince Albert popularized the Christmas tree in the 1840s. The English people knew about Christmas trees before then, but his decision to set up a tree for his family spread the custom.

Early trees included small gifts for family members in addition to decorations. Most decorations at this time were homemade, and many were edible. Glass baubles began to replace homemade decorations around 1860. In the 1870s, the first mass-produced ornaments began to appear. Merchants imported these silver and gold embossed cardboard cutouts from Dresden, Germany. Tinsel icicles made their way over from Nuremberg, Germany in 1878.

The new ornaments quickly became popular. By 1881, Miners' Journal wrote, "So many charming little ornaments can now be bought ready to decorate Christmas trees that it seems almost a waste of time to make them at home."

Edward Johnson claimed to be the first to add electric lights to his tree in 1882. Since he lived within the first square mile of New York City to have electricity, he probably was indeed the first. The fact that he was the Vice President of Edison Electric and could have small bulbs blown and wired in the company laboratory strengthens his claim.

In 1895, electric lights replaced candles on President Cleveland's tree in the White House. Electric lights provided an important innovation, because candles had always been a fire hazard. Often, people lit them only once on Christmas Eve or Christmas Day while buckets of water and towels lay ready around the edges of the room in case of an accident.

In fact, candles were such a fire hazard that in 1908 several insurance companies announced that they would no longer pay for fires started by trees and candles. They considered this a known risk the policy holder took, for which they were not responsible. By 1920, candles had gone completely out of fashion.

The early electric lights were difficult to use, though, because the wiring meant if one light went out, the entire string went out. This led people to arduous searches among scratchy branches, patiently replacing bulb after bulb until they found the culprit. Modern manufacturers wire lights to avoid this problem.

Christmas trees and Jeremiah 10:2-5

People sometimes bring up these verses from Jeremiah when discussing whether or not to have a Christmas tree. In the King James Version they read, "Thus saith the LORD, Learn not the way of the heathen, and be not dismayed at the signs of heaven; for the heathen are dismayed at them. For the customs of the people are vain: for one cutteth a tree out of the forest, the work of the hands of the workman, with the axe. They deck it with silver and with gold; they fasten it with nails and with hammers, that it move not. They are upright as the palm tree, but speak not: they must needs be borne, because they cannot go. Be not afraid of them; for they cannot do evil, neither also is it in them to do good."

At first glance, verse 3 sounds startlingly like a description of a Christmas tree. Those who have a live tree need someone to go to the forest with an axe – or maybe a chainsaw in this modern era – and bring back the tree ready to be decked with ornaments. So does the Bible speak specifically against Christmas trees?

When Jeremiah wrote these verses, Christmas trees were unknown. In the years before Christ, the only possible trees he could have seen were those used in pagan worship. Even so, some say that he wrote prophetically through the guidance of the Holy Spirit, warning future generations against the custom to come and current ones against idolatry.

God is all-knowing and we can't dismiss this possibility lightly. In situations calling for more knowledge, turning to respected commentators for an opinion is wise. Several volumes available on-line at www.biblestudytools.com, with authors like Matthew Henry and Adam Clarke, yielded the same information. Writers addressed idolatry, but made no mention of Christmas trees.

Some suggested comparing this passage with Isaiah 44:9-20, which Jeremiah may have had in mind when he wrote. The description there is more detailed and points strongly to creating an idol, whether out of wood or iron. Setting these verses from Jeremiah in their larger context also point toward idolatry, not Christmas trees.

This begs the question, "can a Christmas tree be an idol?" Anything a person uses to receive comfort and strength, which he or she turns to instead of God, can be an idol. Not as many people in our modern society have physical idols, but many idolize money, status, or power or the things those attributes bring, whether nice houses, cars, or other items. A Christmas tree can become an idol as anything else can if the person putting up a tree chooses to look to it instead of God.

As in deciding all questions (see "Handling Holidays" at the end of the book) people must look to Scripture as a whole and God's individual leading. To many these verses in Jeremiah warn against making an idol and have nothing to do with Christmas. If they make you think of Christmas trees instead, so you can't have a Christmas tree without it being a stumbling block in your faith, then don't put up a tree.

If after considering other opinions, you enjoy a Christmas tree as a seasonal pleasure and find it does not make you think about what draws you away from God, enjoy. The Christmas tree can draw us closer to God through the symbolism people have given it over the years, plus the memories that ornaments and decorations may provide personally.

Whichever choice you make, do so with a heart humbled before God, ready and willing to do His will, and you will be pleasing to Him.

Holly, Ivy, and other Christmas greenery

As with many other symbols, using evergreens seems to be a pre-Christian tradition. People used green wreaths in magical rites to ensure the return of vegetation in the spring. They considered evergreens magical because they remained green when other vegetation lost its leaves. Despite earlier traditions, Christians began using greenery to decorate their homes after persecution ended under Constantine in 313. Celebrants still took care to choose greens that would not make a pagan statement.

Believers adopted holly as a Christian symbol and used it in churches instead of mistletoe. Lists of "magical" plants include holly with other evergreens, but none singled out holly as especially sacred.

Holly reminded Christians of Jesus' crown of thorns. One legend even says holly formed His crown, and the previously white berries turned red when His blood touched them. Either way, the red berries remind Christians of His blood shed for us. Another legend says that the burning bush Moses saw in the wilderness was a holly tree.

Holly became the focus of superstition during the Middle Ages. In England, people believed it had power to protect people from witches. In Germany, a branch of holly from church Christmas decorations brought protection from thunder and lightning to the home. These beliefs, however, grew out of Christian, rather than pagan, custom.

Ivy had been a symbol of the Roman god Bacchus and by extension of unrestrained drinking and eating. The mythological association kept it from becoming a major part of Christmas decorations, though people allowed it to grow on the exterior of homes. Ivy did manage to creep into Christmas through the folk carol "The Holly and the Ivy" which points to a once commonly held belief that holly brought good luck to men and ivy to women.

The first plant used in Christmas decorations, the laurel or bay, now seldom appears. Early Christians in Rome adorned their homes with it to celebrate victory over sin and death as signified by Jesus' birth. In the Roman world, laurel had been a symbol of triumph that translated well into Christian custom.

By the sixteenth century, John Stow was able to write "Against the time of Christmas every man's house, as also their parish churches, were decked with holme, ivie, bayes, and whatsoever the season afforded to be greene." Apparently any pagan associations had diminished enough for greenery to have made its way into both homes and churches.

Mistletoe

One of the plants most clearly connected to pagan customs, the Druids revered mistletoe. The name itself has nothing to do with body parts, but comes from the old Saxon *mistle-tan*. Scholars debate the exact meaning, but it may mean "different branch." The Druids thought mistletoe represented pure spirit because it never touched the earth.

People often gathered mistletoe to celebrate the winter solstice and burned it on the altar in sacrifice. Druids gathered mistletoe by cutting it with a golden knife or sickle and caught it in a clean white cloth. They regarded it as a symbol of future hope and peace. Perhaps the modern custom of kissing under the mistletoe came from a custom of that time. Whenever enemies met under the mistletoe they would drop their weapons and embrace one another.

A Scandinavian legend gives another explanation. The goddess Frigga gave her son, the god Balder, a charm that protected him from anything that sprang from the four elements: earth, air, fire, and water. Loki, who had a grudge against Balder, made an arrow from mistletoe, because it did not come from any of the elements. He gave the arrow to Helder, a blind goddess, who shot it and killed Balder. The combined efforts of all the gods restored Balder to life, and in gratitude Frigga gives a kiss to anyone passing under the mistletoe.

According to old custom, there is etiquette to kissing under the mistletoe. Each time a boy kisses a girl under the mistletoe, he must remove a single berry from the plant. When all berries are gone, the mistletoe loses its power and no more kisses are available.

The church never sanctioned the use of mistletoe because of its origin. Even now people seldom use mistletoe to decorate churches.

Nativity Scenes

When you think of a nativity scene or crèche, you usually think of figurines, not paintings. Christians began illustrating the Nativity not long after it happened. The earliest known picture of the Nativity is a wall decoration from about 380 A.D. found in the burial chamber of a Christian family in St. Sebastian's Catacombs in Rome. Using a manger became part of Christmas celebrations early. Pope Liberius (352-366) may have set up a table-like brick structure to represent the manger in his new church, Santa Maria Maggiore.

Pope Sixtus III (432-440) later renewed and dedicated the basilica to the Virgin. The church's chief treasure was some pieces said to come from the original manger in Bethlehem, which he placed in a side chapel. Mostly likely, worshippers held the first midnight Christmas mass there. Gregory III added to the remembrance in the eighth century when he placed a statue of the Mother and Child there beside the manger, foreshadowing the elaborate scenes to come.

Over the years, the manger became highly decorated, more like a jeweled box than the rustic manger we think of today. Leaders were not trying to create a scene that looked like the actual Nativity, so a decorated manger became a centerpiece for the people in the nativity story. By the year 1000, mangers appeared in most churches at Christmas.

In the thirteenth century, Arnolfo di Cambio sculpted the first nativity scene with freestanding figures for the chapel in the Church of Santa Maria Maggiore. By this time, devotion to Jesus as a baby was so strong in Rome that other churches set up replicas of the manger, too.

These early depictions of the manger were not realistic. They frequently showed an altar-like table with the baby lying on it. As early as the fourth century artists included the ox and donkey to identify the scene, even though Scripture doesn't say they were present at the first Christmas. Isaiah 1:3 states "The ox knows its owner, and the donkey its master's crib, but Israel does not know, my people do not understand."

People generally interpreted this as a Messianic prophecy. Over time, the animals came to have symbolic meaning. The ox represented the Jews, who were under the yoke of the law, while the donkey represented the heathen.

Some early artists painted Jesus lying on sheaves of wheat instead of straw in the manger. Using wheat instead of straw linked the Eucharist, made of wheat, with the body of the Savior.

Pictures led in time to drama. When many people could not read and books were rare, ministers and bishops used other ways to show people the Bible. In the tenth century, the monks of St. Gaul led the growth of new musical forms that lent themselves well to drama. The first church dramas showed the visit of the women to the tomb of Christ. The visit of the shepherds to the manger soon followed.

The first Nativity play was *Officium Pastorum*, the Office of the Shepherds. These early plays were processions of the clergy from place to place in the choir. The first scenes of the shepherds at the manger were silent adoration. Later people added dialog.

They also added characters we might not expect: the two midwives. They were popular characters in early drama and art. People got them from an apocryphal book, the *Protoevangelim of James*. Scholars never considered the book historically accurate, but it was popular and many elements from it became part of how people saw the Nativity.

During the plays, a veiled picture of Mary with Jesus or veiled figures sat on the altar. Two groups of clerics represented the shepherds and the midwives. When the shepherds approached, the midwives asked, "Whom seek ye in the manger?" The shepherds would then reply, "We seek Christ our Lord, a Child wrapped in swaddling clothes according to the angel's word." The midwives would then pull the veil from the picture or figures on the altar, and the shepherd responded with three "Alleluias."

As the plays developed in different areas, they began to become more elaborate. Now an angel guided the shepherds to the manger. As they approached the manger, the shepherds sang "Let us go over to

Bethlehem." They then remained in the choir throughout the remainder of the service. When the service ended, the priest turned to them and asked, "What have you seen, O shepherds, say; tell us what appeared to you on earth." The shepherds responded, "We saw God our Saviour born and round Him the choirs of angels. Alleluia."

The plays reached their full development in the eleventh century. Over time they began to merge. The clergy preferred Magi scenes to the shepherd scenes, since the shepherds sometimes became rowdy, so when the two plays merged, the Magi took precedence. Perhaps this explains why the Magi began appearing at the manger despite the fact that most scholars believe they did not actually appear until as much as two years later.

As the plays grew larger, people began building elaborate sets within the church for the plays. Recall that churches didn't have pews at this time, so there was plenty of room.

They also began using puppets for some characters. In some cases, the puppets performed the entire play. In others, the puppets performed alongside actors. The alternative name for puppet, *marionette*, may come from this tradition. The word means "little Mary" and may come from using puppets for the Virgin Mary at nativity plays and the three Marys at the tomb in Easter plays.

Eventually Herod got his own play, which opened the door for a play about the slaughter of the innocents. As the plays grew, comedic elements entered as well. Scenes at the inn, for example, might display a variety of episodes such as guests drinking, beggars, and servants caring for livestock. The resulting chaos eventually led to church leaders censuring the plays. In 1207 Pope Innocent III wrote a letter to the archbishop of Gniesen denouncing them.

In 1223, St. Francis of Assisi created the first living Nativity scene. He must have been aware of the Pope's letter condemning Nativity dramas, because he wrote to ask permission before setting up his display. Previous displays had been set up inside the church, but St. Francis chose to place his outside. The scenes inside the church used carved figures while St. Francis used people and animals. St. Francis had visited Bethlehem before he set up his scene, so his memories of the actual place may have motivated him.

Later, those following in his footsteps, the Franciscans, popularized the idea over a larger area. Within a hundred years everyone expected their church to have a nativity scene at Christmas. St. Francis also paved the way for craftsmen to make miniature manger scenes for people to use at home.

The crèche began in Naples. The word crèche is French, and may come from the village of Greccio (pronounced Grecho) where St. Francis set up his first crèche. The miniature scenes made of wood or clay began as replicas of the Holy Land. Soon, however, artisans made entire villages in miniature that looked more like their own communities than Bethlehem.

Craftsmen created the first scenes for churches or monasteries. The first in a private home belonged to Constanza Piccolomini di Aragona, Duchess of Amalf. Her elaborate scene had 167 figures and she probably made it before 1567. The craft continued to grow so that at the beginning of the eighteenth century the Christmas crib, or *presepio* in Italian, had developed into a popular art in Naples.

Two very different men, King Carlo III and Gregorio Maria Rocco, a Dominican friar, helped spread the popularity of the scenes. King Carlo loved mechanical devices and enjoyed making elaborate settings for the Nativity scene in his castle. The queen shared his enthusiasm and made costumes for the various figures.

Once the king began devoting time and energy to his Nativity scene, the nobles took up the pastime as well. They competed with each other in making their scenes, and it became fashionable to visit the homes of those who had made especially beautiful ones. In some cases, people illustrated several scenes from the Nativity, not just the manger. Episodes featuring the shepherds, the Magi, and the inn were especially popular. Many later crèches were large enough to fill entire rooms.

The productions featured more than the simple facts of the Biblical stories. Creators put the scenes into contexts the people of the time could understand. At the inn, for example, the viewer might see fish, sausages, and wines from all areas, a countryman unloading a cart, beggars, minstrels playing instruments, and the guests eating and drinking. In addition, they often depicted Naples' nobility at the manger along with people from all other provinces, each dressed correctly with objects he or she might use in daily life.

At the other end of the scale, Brother Gregorio worked among the common people promoting moral and civic improvements. He established the first municipal lighting system in Naples by convincing the citizens to build over a hundred shrines in the darkest corners of the city streets. Votive lamps lit the shrines, and when people came to pray they brought oil to fill them.

He, like St. Francis, held the Nativity story in great reverence and believed that showing the manger scene couldn't help but have a softening effect on even hardened sinners. He began a campaign urging every family in Naples, no matter how poor, to build a *presepio*. When needed, he also helped his parishioners make them.

Around 1800, the tradition spread to the Provence region of France when a group of Italian peddlers from Naples appeared in the streets of Marseilles selling small plaster figures. These *santi belli* included a variety of figures besides the Holy Family as was popular in

Naples. Local artisans liked the figures and began making similar ones called *santon* using pottery clay.

About this time a macaroni-maker named Antoine Maurel wrote a mystery play called *Pastorale* that dramatized how the shepherds learned of Jesus' birth and led the entire village - including other shepherds they met on the way to bring gifts and greetings to the Christ Child. The *santon* makers then added shepherds in a variety of poses to their figures for the crèche.

The tradition in Provence grew much like the Italian one did. The actors in *Pastorale* had worn the clothing of their own era, so the *santon* makers dressed their figures the same, just as figures in Naples represented people of the time. Eventually each maker developed his own series of characters based on the people in his village, which grouped around the Holy Family with the gifts they brought.

As styles changed over time, so did the figures. Looking at a variety of figures through time shows the changes in styles. Artisans in Provence still make *santon* figures today that keep the crèche close to modern reality for those who see it.

In Germany, carved wooden figures became popular. Then, in the late eighteenth century, printers in Augsburg began making heavy paper or cardboard cutouts with manger figures. People could buy the cutouts in color or in black and white and color them by hand. Peddlers even sold a choice of one hundred different paper figures door-to-door during Advent.

In England a different tradition arose. There, families baked a mince pie in the shape of a manger. Often, they placed a figure of the Christ Child in the slight depression on the top. Once served, the pie became an object of devotion as well as part of the meal. When they removed the figure, children gleefully ate the "manger."

The tradition continued until the rise of Puritan influence. They protested mince pies as idolatry and superstition. The Catholics and Anglicans, on the other side, rose to their defense. Eventually, whether or not someone ate mince pie became a test of orthodoxy. When the Puritans took power, they passed legislation prohibiting mince pie as "idolatrie in crust."

Moravians introduced the crèche to America from Germany in the mid-1700s. They called their nativity scene a *putz* from the German word *putzen* (or decorate). By the 1890s, American stores sold plaster and lead nativity figures as well as the materials needed to make crèches.

Another variation of the nativity scene grew in America: the nativity play. Children at Holy Trinity Church in Boston, Massachusetts performed the first nativity play in America during the Christmas season of 1851. The costumed children carried bundles of food, cloth, and other gifts to a crib on the altar, singing Christmas carols as they came.

At the altar a priest received the gifts and later distributed them to the poor. The simple pageant attracted so much attention that the church had to repeat it twice during Christmas week, at the request of Catholic and Protestant alike. The custom spread quickly across the country.

Nativity scenes of all kinds are still popular today. The Italian Fontanini sets, for example, closely follow the traditions of the early Italian *presipios* in style and character selection. Many Christian stores carry olivewood nativities made in Israel, while catalogs and other stores feature the nativity in a variety of possibilities from an Indian teepee to snowmen.

Poinsettias

With its red and green foliage, the poinsettia is a perfect symbol for Christmas. People in Mexico call it the "flower of the holy night." Mexican legend tells of a village with a custom of placing gifts for the Christ child before the crèche in the church on Christmas Eve. A small boy with nothing to give knelt to pray in the snow outside. When he rose, a beautiful plant with scarlet leaves grew where he knelt. He then presented it as his gift for the Christ child.

The Aztec Indians cultivated the poinsettia for centuries and used it to make a reddish-purple dye. The first reported use as part of Christmas celebrations was by Franciscan priests near Taxco, Mexico in the seventeenth century. Joel R. Poinsett, the first American minister to Mexico introduced the poinsettia to America.

Contrary to popular belief, poinsettias are not poisonous. That rumor started in 1919 when a doctor in Hawaii erroneously attributed a child's death to eating a poinsettia leaf. Recent studies have shown that the leaves are not lethal and a 1995 study of data from poison control centers found no toxic reactions out of almost 23,000 reported exposures to the plant.

Santa Claus

Santa Claus had his beginning in St. Nicholas, bishop of Myra in Asia Minor during the first half of the fourth century. His is an odd story. Other customs began with non-Christian sources to which people added Christian meaning. Santa Claus is a case of the opposite: a strongly Christian beginning with a secular ending. (See St. Nicholas' Day for more information.)

The German Reformation began the change from St. Nicholas to Santa Claus. Luther wanted to de-emphasize the saints, but he knew that people would object to losing the gift-giving tradition associated with St. Nicholas. So instead of banning the day, he gave it a twist. Children now received gifts from Jesus, who gave them on His own birthday.

A certain amount of theology lay behind the decision to change the name. Reformers wanted to encourage everyone, not just children, to stop looking to the various saints for help and rely instead on Christ. As one early Protestant pastor said, "the holy Christ Child gives us all good things for body and soul, and He alone it is whom we ought to call upon."

German children began looking forward to the visit of the *Christkindl* or Christ child. Once in America, the German pronunciation of *Christkindl* (both i's are short) became Anglicized as "Kriss Kringle," and adopted as Santa's other name. The change did not go unnoticed or unopposed. Rev. A. B. Grosh wrote in the Christian Ambassador in 1854:

"'Kriss Kringle' - This horridly barbarous imitation of a German barbarism, into which an English ear has led many of our newspaper editors and writers. Christ-kindler, or Christ-kinchen, is the German proper for Christ-child, or infant Christ. Many Germans have corrupted it into Christ-kintle - particularly in Pennsylvanian. This is bad enough, but to corrupt it still more, and remove it utterly away from all semblance to the original is too bad. 'Kriss Kringle' as a name for the 'Babe of Bethlehem' is neither English nor bad German, but a mere jargon or gibberish of the vilest kind - and when the facts are known, sounds like ribaldry. I hope that religious papers, at least, will cease from, and steadily discountenance such seeming profanity of the name of Christ. Use the German names - any of them - but avoid 'Kriss Kringle'."

If not for several different pieces of literature, Santa might have remained more a religious than a secular figure. Or at least, he might have remained a regional part of Christmas rather than a general one. However, in 1809 Washington Irving continually mentioned St. Nicholas in his *Diedrich Knickerbocker's History of New York from the Beginning of the World to the End of the Dutch Dynasty*. This introduced St. Nicholas to many who had never heard of him. Secularization also began, since Irving presented him as a pipe-smoking Dutchman rather than as a bishop.

The process continued with the publication of Clement Clark Moore's poem "A Visit from St. Nicholas." Moore was an acquaintance of Irving's and was of Dutch ancestry himself. He later said that he had modeled his version of St. Nick on a "portly rubicund Dutchman" who had lived near his father's home. In addition, he took characteristics from other of the individuals in Irving's history and gave them to St. Nicholas.

Moore first shared the poem with his children on December 23, 1822. He didn't want to publish it, as he felt with would damage his reputation as a serious scholar. A friend of the family who had read the poem sent a copy of it to *The Troy Sentinel*, where it published on December 23, 1823, a year after its creation. Moore didn't claim the poem as his until 1844 when he finally included it in a collection of his works.

Though he had borrowed many elements from Irving's work, he added many touches of his own. Even though he titled the poem "A Visit from St. Nicholas," the Santa legend had been born. He established most of the familiar elements of Santa Claus within it.

Two books published in 1842 and 1845 respectively, *Kriss Kringle's Book* and *Kriss Kringle's Christmas Tree*, both helped spread Santa's popularity and completed the merge of the *Christkindl* with Santa Claus. *Kriss Kringle's Christmas Tree* holds another distinction. The illustration on the title page may show Santa Claus and the Christmas tree together for the first time in this country. The tree bears little resemblance to today's Christmas tree, as it appears to be a deciduous tree complete with leaves. The picture shows Santa hanging toys from his pack on the tree.

Santa's elves appeared as early as 1856. Louisa May Alcott wrote, but didn't publish, a book titled *Christmas Elves*. Elves or some kind of mythical helpers were a natural addition to a fairy tale like Santa. An engraving in Godey's Lady's Book from 1873 shows the elves in Santa's workshop. The elves got additional recognition in 1876 when Edward Eggleston wrote *The House of Santa Claus, a Christmas Fairy Show for Sunday Schools*.

Santa even appeared on money. In 1858 the Howard Banking Company of Boston, Massachusetts issued a $5.00 bill for the Christmas season. This was before the United States developed a standard U.S. currency, when individual banks issued their own money. The bill shows a Dutch-looking Santa driving off of a snow covered rooftop in his reindeer-drawn sleigh as he looks back to the chimney.

Thomas Nast, head editorial cartoonist at Harper's Weekly from 1860-1890, continued to popularize and embellish the Santa Claus story with his drawings. His first illustration of Santa Claus appeared in 1862. At this time, Clement Clark Moore's poem already in existed, and Nast probably knew it. Some elements in his illustrations came from Moore's poem, but he added many of his own embellishments.

Among other things, he added Santa's home at the North Pole and established that Santa uses a telescope to see whether children are good or bad. He also showed Santa's book recording good and bad children, and gave glimpses of Santa's home life. Nast's grandson later claimed that he chose the North Pole for Santa's home because it was equidistant from most countries in the Northern Hemisphere.

Santa Claus, as we know him today, also contains many elements of the Norse god, Thor, whom artists showed as a large, elderly man with a long white beard. People considered Thor a cheerful and friendly god who always helped people. According to legend, Thor lived in the "North-land" where he had his palace among icebergs.

Thor's element was fire and his color was red. The fireplace was especially sacred to him, and many stories said he came down the chimney into the fire. These sound like Santa Claus. Clement Clark Moore and Thomas Nast may have used these elements of Norse mythology to shape their visions of Santa Claus.

The Thor element remained clear for a time. In 1897 a Macy's advertisement showed Santa dressed like the warrior god. During the same time period a German clockwork toy showed Santa riding in Thor's chariot pulled by two reindeer. Another had Santa's sleigh drawn by Thor's team of goats.

Another source gave a different story of why Santa comes down the chimney. Hertha or Bertha was a Norse goddess of domesticity and the home. People decorated their houses with fir and evergreens to welcome her coming during the winter solstice. When the family gathered to eat, they built an altar of flat stores and laid a fire with fir boughs. Hertha descended through the smoke to bless the home. Santa's habit of coming down the chimney instead of entering through the door may be the only survival of this tradition.

Yet another source gave Santa's habit of descending the chimney a Scottish origin. There people hung rowan branches over doors and windows to protect themselves from fairies and witches. Since Santa was a type of fairy, he couldn't pass the rowan and had to come down the chimney.

For a long time, Santa Claus had his own magazine. *St. Nicholas* magazine remained in publication from 1873 to 1940, with further issues released in 1943. The magazine helped begin and continue the popularization of Santa Claus, and established the identification of St. Nicholas with Santa.

The magazine wasn't just for Christmas, but was the premier children's literary periodical of the nineteenth century. Over the years contributors included such outstanding authors as Louisa May Alcott, Frances Hodgson Burnett, Mark Twain, Robert Louis Stevenson, and Rudyard Kipling. Many classic children's books first appeared in the pages of *St. Nicholas* before their official release.

Children began writing letters to Santa as early as 1874. The idea apparently spread quickly. Children flooded the post office with letters by the 1890s.

The first of the familiar department store Santas appeared in 1890. James Edgar, a store owner in Brockton, Massachusetts, had tried a variety of costumes to get parents to bring children in the store. A clown, war heroes, and Uncle Sam brought limited success. When he dressed as Santa, children flocked into the store. His success spread and now you can find Santa at department stores and malls around America.

Mrs. Claus made her debut in 1899 in a book titled *Goody Santa Claus on a Sleigh Ride*. The book was one of thirty-two written by Katharine Lee Bates, better known as the composer of "America the Beautiful." *Goody* was a contraction of "Good Wife," an early New England term used instead of Mrs.

No one is sure when children began leaving food for Santa. In 1908 the New York Tribune told its readers how children in one family left out a lunch for Santa. They had reasoned that he would be tired after all his hard work. The children set the table, ground coffee, and left out covered sandwiches and cake. The next morning the food was gone and they found a note pinned to the Christmas tree thanking them for their kindness.

At one time, children also left out carrots or hay for Santa's reindeer. Children in the country, who knew what animals needed, left piles of salt on their windowsills for them. The next morning, a smudged window and the absence of the salt told them Santa and his reindeer arrived during the night.

A marketing campaign made Santa Claus the figure we know today. In 1930 Coca-Cola adopted him as their trademark for a time, and artist Haddon Sundbloom's portrayal of him as a plump, jolly, red-cheeked man became the popular image.

The only major piece missing from the Santa myth was a special reindeer named Rudolph. A publication called *The Children's Friend* first mentioned Santa's reindeer in 1821, "Old Sante Claus with much delight, His reindeer drives this frosty night." Clement Clark Moore gave the reindeer names in his poem. Robert May added Rudolph the Red Nosed Reindeer to the group in 1939. A copywriter for Montgomery Ward, May wrote the story as a giveaway for the department store Santas.

During the initial run in 1939, the store gave away 2.4 million copies. They used the book again in 1946 and gave away 3.6 million. After the second printing, Ward's returned the copyright to May, who found a publisher and sold 100,000 copies the first year. In 1949 May and his brother-in-law Johnny Marks turned the story into a song. Gene Autry recorded the song and Rudolph became a permanent part of the Santa story.

Xmas

Probably one of the most misunderstood customs is abbreviating Christmas by writing Xmas. Some seem to feel that in doing so, people are attempting to "x-out" Christ. Actually, Xmas is a true abbreviation of the word "Christmas." In Greek, the first letter of Christ's name is chi, written in Greek as X. The equivalent to Xmas, transliterated completely into English, would be Chimas or C'mas, abbreviating Christ's name rather than writing out the word. The Oxford English Dictionary mentions a longer version, X'temmas, dating from 1551. Another source indicated that people may have used the abbreviation as early as the twelfth century.

Yule

Though now used as an alternate name for Christmas, Yule was originally from a German-Celtic feast at the beginning of November. People knew the feast by various names, including *Jiuleis* or *Guili*, but as Yule in Scandinavia. After the Roman conquest, the feast moved to the winter solstice which placed it where it could become associated with Christmas.

The word may have come from the Gothic *quil* or *hiul*, meaning wheel and referring to the wheel of the year - the annual revolution of the sun. Another possibility is the Gothic *ol* or *oel* and the Anglo-Saxon *geol*, meaning feast and the liquor drunk at the feast.

People celebrated the original Yule with drinking, feasting, and fertility rites. As part of the celebration, they burned oak logs to honor the god Thor. He was the enemy of demons, but a friend to man.

The Yule log is probably a leftover from this winter solstice custom. A bonfire was a common feature of the celebration, just as it was at midsummer. Revelers brought in the Yule log of oak, pine, ask, or birch with ivy-covered ropes, children sitting astride it. In Great Britain, before the Christmas tree became part of Christmas, the Yule log played a major role in celebrations.

Usually people kindled the Yule log on Christmas Eve with remnants of the previous year's log. According to some, the log should burn the entire twelve days of Christmas. Others said you only had to light it daily until Twelfth night. If the log went out by itself, you could expect bad luck. Once Christmas was over, householders removed the log and kept it under a bed as protection against fire and thunder.

Christmas Music

Carols are one of the most familiar and joyful parts of Christmas. Most people consider all Christmas songs to be Christmas carols. Technically speaking the older ballads handed down from generation to generation with no known composer are the only true carols. The other songs are hymns. They have specific composers and are more elaborate musically. Like the rest of the American Christmas celebration, our carols reflect a variety of different origins.

Early Latin Hymns

Latin hymns for church worship became the first Christmas music. We have examples as old as the fourth century. Modern listeners would find them stiff and formal, as they focused more on the theological part of Christmas. Writers made no attempt to imagine the stable or see Jesus as a real baby.

Two examples show the theological nature of these hymns. "Veni, redemptor gentium" is one of the earliest Latin hymns and one of the few existing from Ambrose, Archbishop of Milan, considered to be the father of Church song.

"Veni, redemptor gentium,	Come, Redeemer of the nations,
Ostende partum virginis;	Show the virgin's offspring;
Miretur omne saeculum:	Every generation will adore Him
Talis decet partus Deum.	As befits the offspring of God.
Non ex virili semine,	Not of human seed begotten,
Sed mystico spiramine,	But of mystic Spirit,
Verbum Dei factum caro,	Word of God made flesh,
Fructusque ventris floruit.	And fruit of the womb blossomed."

The second, "Corde natus ex Parentis" ("Of the Father's love begotten") came from a longer hymn by Spanish poet Prudentius (c. 348-413). He didn't write it for the liturgy, so the church didn't adopt it for several centuries. Still, the focus is entirely on the abstract rather than on the human aspects of the Nativity.

Ante mundi exordium,	Before the beginning of the universe,
Alpha et O cognominatus,	Alpha and Omega he was named,
Ipse fons et clausula	Himself beginning and end
Ominum quae sunt, fuerunt,	Of all things which are, which have been,
Quaeque post futura sunt	And which will be
Saeculorum saeculis.	From generation to generation."

Macaronic Carols

Though secular carols existed earlier, the first religious carols date back to the late thirteenth or the fourteenth century. The word carol originally referred to a dance, usually a ring dance, often with words that indicated actions. People used secular carols for joyful, exuberant celebrations.

This joy began to spill over into the popular culture's celebration of Christmas. Composers used the language of each country instead of Latin for these carols. Also, they began focusing on the human side of the nativity: the emotions of the participants or the lowly surroundings.

Early macaronic carols provided a bridge between the church Latin hymns and popular music. Carol writers inserted fragments of Latin texts into lyrics written in their own language. Sometimes the Latin was only a word or two, while in other carols entire lines in Latin alternated with every day speech. The familiar "Good Christian Men, Rejoice" is an English translation of a German song of this type. We still know the tune by the same name as the Latin text: *In Dulci Jubilio.*

"In dulci jubilo
Nu singet und set fro!
Unsers Herzen wonne
Leyt in praesepio
Und leuchtet als die Sonne
Matris in gremio.
Alpha es et O!"

After the macaronic carols, most of the later English carols were some type of ballad, though still carols because they were folk songs without known composers. In general, people heard and sang the "traditional" carols from the fifteenth to the eighteenth centuries.

St. Francis and the carols

People often credit St. Francis of Assisi with popularizing or even creating Christmas carols. Accounts of the first crèche say that he burst into joyful song when he saw the people's response. Carol singing became part of the later crèche celebrations throughout Italy.

One of his disciples, Jacopone di Todi receives credit for writing the first Christmas songs in Italian. He and other Franciscans wanted to help people see the human aspects of the gospel while not forgetting the divine.

Some of the Italian carols seem to have shaped how we view the nativity today. Many nativity scenes show baby Jesus lying nearly naked on the hay with His arms stretched out instead of wrapped in swaddling clothes as Scripture says. This idea came from the Italian emphasis on the poverty and simplicity of His birth.

Portions of two carols, both by Jacopone, show this clearly:

"Come and look upon her child
Nestling in the hay!
See his fair arms opened wide,
On her lap to play!"

"In the worthy stable of the sweet baby
the angels are singing round the little one;
they sing and cry out, the beloved angels,
quite reverent, timid and shy
round the little baby Prince of the Elect
who lies naked among the prickly hay."

German Carols

German carols began to develop slightly later in the fourteenth century, partially because of Eckhart of Strasburg's preaching. A Dominican, he focused on the Divine Birth in the soul of a believer. This led to a greater focus on the physical birth of Jesus at Christmas as well.

Following the pattern of other carols, they focused more on the human emotions in the Nativity. *Hirtenlieder* or shepherd songs were particularly popular. The rural people identified with the shepherds of Bethlehem and tried to share their emotions at the first Christmas. Refrains often imitated shepherds' instruments.

Another mainly German carol was the companion carol. The singer in this type carol imagined himself accompanying the shepherds or others to visit Baby Jesus. Composers wrote in local dialects to add familiarity in the song.

Personal religion rather than theological doctrine is stronger in German music than in any other. The German Reformation gave rise to some of the best Christmas hymns. Unlike the English Reformation, the German Reformation did not restrict celebrating Christmas. Martin Luther wrote some carols while Paul Gerhardt, a seventeenth century Berlin pastor, wrote others.

We consider their music hymns because we know the composer, but both men believed in using popular melodies for their messages. In all of his hymn writing, not just Christmas hymns, Luther believed in using common language to make ideas accessible to anyone. One contemporary lamented, "Luther's hymns have destroyed more souls than his writings and speeches."

One of Luther's best known hymns is actually not his. People often refer to "Away in a Manger" as "Luther's Cradle Hymn" but he wrote neither words nor music. The second part of the first stanza of Luther's hymn "Vom Himmel Kam der Engel Schar" may have inspired the composer of "Away in the Manger." This line, in English, reads "Away there in the manger a little Infant lies."

The familiar English text is American, probably written by German Lutherans in Pennsylvania. The poem first appeared in print in Philadelphia in 1885. The tie to Luther's hymn and the fact that a Lutheran wrote it may have resulted in the confusion over authorship.

French Noels

French carols developed about the same time as the English carols. The French Noel focused on Christmas, and carolers repeated the word "noel" as part of the refrain. The familiar tune to "O Come, O Come, Emmanuel" is from a fifteenth century French Noel.

We're uncertain of the French noel's origin. It may have its roots in the Latin *natalis* or birthday. The other possibility is from the old English word *nowell*, which means news. Writers used noel in carols in the sense of bringing news, as in "The First Noel." Both may be correct. The two words *noel* and *nowell* had different origins, but they came to mean the same thing because people pronounced them the same.

Ballad Carols

A ballad is a simple poem telling a popular story in short stanzas, but we can divide ballad carols into different types. Many are Nativity ballads. They tell the story of Jesus' birth, often from different points of view. The familiar "God Rest Ye Merry, Gentlemen" is a nativity ballad written from the point of view of the shepherds who are telling the Good News.

Legendary or mystery carols are another group. These focus on different legends surrounding the Nativity. Some may go back to Apocryphal stories retold in song. One of the best known, at least in England, is "The Cherry Tree," the first two stanzas of which follow.

"Joseph was an old man,
And an old man was he,
When he wedded Mary
in the land of Galilee.

Joseph and Mary walked
Through an orchard good,
Where was cherries and berries
As red as any blood"

Lullabies in which the writer imagines words Mary might have sung while cradling her baby are another type of ballad carol. Mary herself shows up in many carols. Before the Reformation, a large body of *Marienlieder* songs became popular. These songs focused on Mary rather than on her Son. After the Reformation, people adapted many of these to the new focus by substituting Jesus' name for Mary's.

An example we still sing today is "Lo How a Rose E'er Blooming." In the days before the Reformation, people frequently referred to Mary as "the blooming branch" or "the rose without thorns" among other names. After the Reformation, the focus of this German carol changed to Jesus, instead of Mary.

"Lo, how a Rose e'er blooming
From tender stem hath sprung!
Of Jesse's lineage coming
As men of old have sung.
It came a floweret bright,
Amid the cold of winter,
When half-spent was the night.

Isaiah 'twas foretold it,
The rose I have in mind;
With Mary we behold it,
The virgin mother kind.
To show God's love aright
She bore to men a Saviour,
When half-spent was the night."

Perhaps what the editors had in mind when they reworked the carol were these verses from Isaiah. "The wilderness and the solitary place shall be glad for them; and the desert shall rejoice, and blossom as the rose. It shall blossom abundantly, and rejoice even with joy and singing: the glory of Lebanon shall be given unto it, the excellency of Carmel and Sharon, they shall see the glory of the LORD, and the excellency of our God." Isaiah 35:1. (KJV) The original identification of Mary with the rose has changed so Jesus is Himself the Rose.

Prayer carols are quite similar to lullabies. In these, the singer addresses Jesus directly with wonder, devotion, and admiration.

Carols were not just for Christmas. People sang doctrinal carols that focused on other parts of Redemption. Some people sang these at Christmas as well. Focusing on Christ's entire life, not just His birth, became common during the Christmas season.

Number carols are an unusual variety of ballad carol. "The Seven Joys of Mary" is probably the most familiar of this type, but all use numbers to tell a story. The familiar children's song "This Old Man" is a secular number carol. "The Twelve Days of Christmas" is later than most traditional carols, but would fit into this type.

The last two types of ballad carols are secular rather than sacred, but are still a part of our celebration. The first are wassail carols such as "Here we come a caroling." The original wording, sometimes still heard today, was "Here we come a wassailing." These were purely fun songs used during feudal days when vassals expected their upper class masters to share food and drink at Christmas.

The final type is the folklore carol. These deal with traditional elements of the Christmas celebration that are not necessarily Christian. "The Holly and the Ivy" is a folklore carol reflecting traditions associated with the two plants. Like other early carols, the symbolism may go back to pre-Christian traditions.

The medieval mystery plays gave carols an additional boost. Christmas was a popular theme for the various plays. As they developed, composers wrote more and more music to go along with them.

Carols fell out of favor in England after 1647 and the Puritan Commonwealth. The new government forbade carols and mystery plays along with all other parts of the Christmas celebration. When the monarchy was restored, carols gradually regained favor, though not to the same level as before.

Christmas Hymns

The eighteenth century saw the rise of Christmas hymns. With the decline of carols, new music needed to fill the gap. Some composers went back to earlier poems to find lyrics for their new hymns. Therefore, even though we consider the hymn to be eighteenth-century, the lyrics are older.

Isaac Watts' hymnbooks were the first to receive wide circulation. Of his, the most important was *Hymns and Spiritual Songs*, published in 1707. Others followed.

English carols received a rebirth in the nineteenth century. People began making efforts to find and preserve old carols before they died out. In 1833, William Sandys released *Selection of Christmas Carols, Ancient and Modern*. J. M. Neale's *Carols for Christmastide* followed in 1852. The process of recording and publishing carols brought them back. In combination with a new emphasis on Christmas, thanks to the popularization of the Christmas tree and Christmas cards, carols made a comeback.

The confusion between hymns and carols is fairly recent. The first hymnbook to include both was most likely the *Oxford Hymn Book of 1908*. *Congregational Hymnary* had eleven carols separate from the hymns in 1916.

Christmas Music in America

The older hymns and carols are still favorites today. As with other traditions, Christmas music in America is a blend from various countries. We have inherited some of the best from around the world, but we have added our own touches.

A missionary to the Huron Indians, John de Brebeuf wrote the first American carol. He worked among the Hurons until 1626 when the Iroquois captured and killed him. Appropriately for a carol, he wrote it in the Huron language and modeled it after a sixteenth century French folk song. The Hurons preserved *Jesous Ahatonnia* (Jesus is Born) and a later missionary wrote it down.

In translation, here are the words to the first American carol:

"O, harken to the angels' word,
Do not decline
To heed the message which you heard:
The Child Divine,
As they proclaim, has come this morn
Of Mary pure, Let us adore.
Jesus is born."

America has added popular Christmas hymns to the standard list. During the nineteenth century, revival and the growth of Christmas customs spurred new music. Familiar American Christmas hymns include "It Came Upon the Midnight Clear" written in 1876 by Edmund H. Sears, a Unitarian minister from Weston Massachusetts.

Phillips Brooks wrote "O Little Town of Bethlehem" after a visit to Israel where he visited the site of the Nativity. The organist of Holy Trinity Church in Philadelphia, where Brooks was then rector, wrote the tune in 1865. Children in the Sunday School sang the hymn for the first time on Christmas 1868.

Secular Christmas music developed at the same time. Unitarian clergyman John Pierpont of Boston wrote "Jingle Bells" in 1856. In 1863, Godey's Lady's Book announced the forthcoming release of new music for the season.

As musical styles have changed in America, Christmas music has changed along with them. "Santa Claus is Coming to Town" made an appearance in 1934. A musical setting for "'Twas the Night Before Christmas" came out at the end of the 1930s. Both foreshadowed the coming boom in secular Christmas music.

Though composers had written and released new Christmas music before, 1942 heralded the real birth of secular Christmas music in

America. Bing Crosby sang "White Christmas" in *Holiday Inn*, and won an Oscar in 1942. Since then people have bought over thirty million copies of the song and artists from all genres have recorded it.

The popularity of "White Christmas" set the standard for much of the new Christmas music. Home and nostalgia became familiar themes for most new releases. World War II may have been a factor as homesick GIs remembered Christmases past.

The trend continued in 1944 when Judy Garland sang "Have Yourself a Merry Little Christmas" in *Meet Me in St. Louis*. Every year thereafter through the end of the decade saw the addition of a song now considered part of the accepted list of Christmas songs. In 1945, "Let It Snow, Let It Snow, Let It Snow!" joined the group, and in 1946 the warm and cozy "The Christmas Song (Chestnuts Roasting on an Open Fire)" debuted.

"Here Comes Santa Claus" in 1947 did more than add a new song to the list. Both it and the later "Rudolph the Red-Nosed Reindeer" were among the first to use pictures on the record sleeve as a marketing tool. Shrewd producers considered that a cartoon picture of Santa on the cover would make a child to beg for the record, resulting in added sales for the company. Before long, color covers were a regular part of the industry.

Novelty songs began to appear at the end of the 1940s and into the 1950s. While we might consider some of the earlier songs novelties, composers intended them for children. The newer novelty songs amused an adult audience. "All I Want for Christmas (Is My Two Front Teeth)" was the first, in 1948.

"Rudolph the Red-Nosed Reindeer" moved from children's book to song in 1949. Not only did it contribute to a new marketing strategy, it holds a dubious distinction as setting a new trend for Christmas as a marketing vehicle in general. "Rudolph" owed its entire existence to marketing, from the first book to the song and later TV special.

In 1950 "Frosty the Snow Man" followed into the history of Christmas. The television special came much later, in 1969. Novelty still reigned with "I Saw Mommy Kissing Santa Claus" in 1952 and "Nuttin' for Christmas" in 1955. "Sweet Little Jesus Boy" also came out in 1955, showing that composers had not completely forgotten the sacred.

"Mary's Boy Child" arrived in 1956, while 1957 featured the arrival of "Jingle Bell Rock." The flood of music began to slow toward the end of the '50s and the coming of the '60s. Only a few more songs became part of the common music heard at Christmas.

In 1958 "The Little Drummer Boy" took his place as a Christmas icon. Like others, the song eventually became a TV special, in 1968 and 1976. A totally different song, "Rockin' Around the Christmas Tree" released in 1958 as well. Finally, "Winter Wonderland" entered the scene in 1964.

With the 1960s, music began to segment into different styles. Christmas music was no longer as important, and most albums featured new renditions of older music rather than completely new songs. Those featuring new music seldom reached beyond the particular style's market. Today the market waits for another new song that will break out of its genre to become the latest addition to Christmas in America.

The growth of both Gospel and contemporary Christian music added more titles to the list of choices in Christmas music. While compilers have not included these in more traditional hymnals, the newer hymnals that focus on praise and worship styles have begun to add modern Christmas music.

Even though the hymnals may not yet feature contemporary Christmas music, some titles are beginning to move into traditional circles. People sing "Mary Did you Know" by Mark Lowery and Buddy Greene in both traditional and progressive churches.

For contemporary Christian and gospel music lovers, most popular artists release a Christmas album. These tend to feature a mix of old and new. Artists may give older songs a more contemporary setting in keeping with the artists' style. New songs specifically written for Christmas may debut on each release.

If Christmas is your favorite time of year, you're in good company. The rich traditions of the season make it special for many. As Christians, we have the best of both worlds: rich and varied traditions set into the knowledge that God sent us a Savior. For us, the heart of the season is Immanuel: God with us.

HANDLING

HOLIDAYS

So, whether you eat or drink, or whatever you do, do all to the glory of God.
1 Corinthians 10:31

Christians have been asking how to handle holidays since the beginning of the faith. Unfortunately, Paul wasn't inspired to write I and II Holidays outlining exactly what holidays Christians should celebrate and how we should celebrate them. Because of this, holidays fall into the gray area of our faith. Unless Scripture specifically contradicts part of a celebration, each of us must decide how to handle celebrations.

Paul dealt with a similar situation when he wrote about the problem of meat sacrificed to idols in I Corinthians 8-10. Believers weren't sure whether or not Christians could eat this meat and please to God. Paul left the matter to the believer's conscience. In doing so, he also left some good guidelines for us in deciding about current customs.

Where we often go astray in thinking about the matter is in asking whether or not we may participate in a holiday or custom. Paul makes it clear that Christians have freedom to do anything, though not everything is beneficial. Based on I Corinthians 8-10, we must ask three questions. First, does it glorify God? Second, is it beneficial to my walk with God? Third, will it make someone else stumble in his or her walk?

The third question can be the hardest. While a choice may not bother us, God calls us to be careful that our choices not confuse or lead astray another believer with a more tender conscience. On the other hand, the believer with the tender conscience should not use this to control another believer's choices. Choosing to love your brothers and sisters more than your own pleasure lies at the heart of this Scripture, whether your conscience is firm or tender.

Since we do have freedom, celebrations may look as different as each individual. God gives each of us the Holy Spirit as a guide to deciding how we understand different Scriptural guidelines. We may all make different choices and disagree with some of the choices others make.

So what are the different possibilities to handling holidays and holiday customs? They range from completely accepting and celebrating a holiday, through a modified or possibly alternative celebration, to not celebrating at all.

Centuries divide the modern customs from the original ones. If you decide that the modern custom is harmless, then you may choose to participate in a holiday. The issue in deciding is to hold each custom against the measure of Scripture. Since the definition of "beneficial" depends on your conscience, our answers will probably be quite different.

For example, after learning more about the origins of Halloween, if you no longer see the "haunted" aspect of the holiday as innocent fun, you may want to participate in a different way. Consider decorating with fall fruits and vegetables instead of a carved Jack O'Lantern. Carving a pumpkin with Christian symbols is another possibility.

On the other end of the spectrum is deciding that because of the pagan associations with a given holiday, you should not participate in the holiday at all. If after prayer and consideration you don't feel comfortable with any custom, you shouldn't participate in the holiday.

Despite our disagreements we need to accept the choices other believers make. Through the years, Christians have found many things to cause division. Now, more than ever, we need to show the world the love the Lord gives us for each other, even when we disagree.

A closer look at this passage in I Corinthians helps in this matter. Paul could have answered the question with yes or no. Instead, he went deeper and looked at what benefited others, not just himself. Love becomes the bottom line.

Consider your choices prayerfully. Consult the Bible for guidance. Then celebrate each holiday with a clear conscience – or don't celebrate at all – knowing your choice will be pleasing to God.

Children and Holidays

While the same basic guidelines on making decisions work for children and adults, the question of handling holidays for children is a little different. Children aren't miniature adults. They don't think like adults and don't process information like adults do. Because of this, parents need to take care when making decisions involving their children. A child may have a more tender conscience than an adult does, because he or she does not yet have the "filters" adults do. Things that don't bother an adult may give problems to a child.

Children are also learning. They don't have the background adults do, especially when it comes to the Bible. They can't balance what they see and hear with other information. Because they are not as far along in learning to know God, parents should be more cautious.

Children have difficulty separating fantasy from reality and think on a concrete level. We must be careful, therefore, that we do not put the real things of God on a level with those from the fantasy world. While Santa kneeling at the manger can be a meaningful symbol for adults, a child will take both as equally real.

Instead of teaching the abstract lesson that the things of the world must bow to those of God, we may have put confusion in the child's mind, as they see Santa Claus and Jesus presented on the same level of reality. Telling the child that one is real and one is fantasy when he or she sees both pictured together may only add to the confusion. Seeing Santa at every shopping mall doesn't help understand the difference, either.

If you're thinking that your child can understand the difference if you explain it carefully, consider this example.

As a child, I remember clearly arguing with my first grade teacher and my mother that 1-1=1. The problem wasn't my teacher's explanation of subtraction. The physical problem on paper kept me from understanding the concept behind it.

Because I saw two 1s written on the paper, I believed that if you covered up one of the 1s, you would still one of them left. Therefore, 1-1=1. It's a classic example of how a child can take something simple to an adult and misunderstand it.

I don't remember when I finally understood that 1-1=0, but I remember being unconvinced by the teacher's attempt to explain that it was the same 1 when I saw two of them written down.

As a parent, use holidays to teach. For young children, this will be mainly by example. What you do sets an example for your child. As children grow older, you can use holidays to teach the principles you use to make decisions about them. You may change how you celebrate as your children get older.

Remember, too, that children are as different as adults are. God gives each of us a unique personality at the very beginning. Not only do children understand differently simply because they are children, each child has different sensitivities. You may come up with different answers for different children.

While you don't want to overload children with information or ask them to understand differences beyond their years, don't be shy in giving explanations. Even a holiday you do not celebrate can be a teaching opportunity.

Trying to explain holidays to children can be difficult. It can also be hard to come up with our own alternatives to holidays if you choose not to participate in all or part of one.

Whatever you decide, do it to the glory of God. Holidays began as holy days, so there's no reason they can't still be holy. While people look at the outward appearance, God looks at the heart. If you approach your celebration with a desire to honor God, then whatever you do is acceptable.

Susan E. Richardson

References

-----*American Holidays and Special Days*, Maryland Historical Press, Lanham, MD, 1986.

----*Christmas in Colonial and Early America*, World Book, Inc. Chicago, IL 1996.

----*Dictionary of the Middle Ages*, Scribner's, New York, 1984.

----Encyclopedia Britannica, Encyclopedia Britannica, Inc., 1978.

----*Reader's Digest Book of Christmas*, Pleasantville, NY: Readers Digest Association, 1985.

----*Thanksgiving Primer*. Plymouth, MA: Plimoth Plantation, 1987.

----*The Time Life Book of Christmas*. New York: Prentice Hall Press, 1987.

Achen, Sven Tito. *Symbols around Us*. New York: Van Nostrand Reinhold Company, 1978.

Anwyl, E., *Celtic Religion in Pre-Christian Times*. n.p.: n.d. Kindle edition.

Appelbaum, Diana Karter. *Thanksgiving: An American Holiday, an American History*. New York: Facts on File Publications, 1984.

Bamford, Christopher, and Marsh, William Peter, ed. *Celtic Christianity*. Great Barrington, MA: Lindisfarne Press, 1987.

Bannatyne, Lesley Pratt. *Halloween: An American Holiday, an American History*. Gretna, LA: Pelican Publishing Co., 1990.

Barth, Edna. *Lilies, Rabbits, and Painted Eggs: The Story of the Easter Symbols*. New York: Seabury Press, 1970.

Barth, Edna. *Shamrocks, Harps, and Shillelaghs*. New York: Clarion Books, 1977.

Baur, John E. *Christmas on the American Frontier.* Caldwell, ID: The Caxton Printers, Ltd., 1961.

Becker, May Lamberton. *The Home Book of Christmas.* New York: Dodd, Mead and Company, 1941.

Bennett, Margaret. *Scottish Customs.* Edinburgh: Birlinn Limited, 2004.

Biedermann, Hans. *Dictionary of Symbolism.* New York: Facts on File, Inc., 1992.

Black, Jeremy, and Green, Anthony. *Gods, Demons and Symbols of Ancient Mesopotamia.* Austin, TX: University of Texas Press, 2003.

Bradshaw, Paul F., and Johnson, Maxwell E., *The Origins of Feasts, Fasts and Seasons in Early Christianity.* Collegeville, MN: Liturgical Press, 2011.

Cade, Sharon. *Special Days: History, Folklore, and Whatnot.* Portland, OR: SC Enterprises, 1984.

Chevalier, Jean, and Gheerbrant, Alain. *The Penguin Dictionary of Symbols.* New York: Penguin Group, 1996.

Chris, Teresa. *Story of Santa Claus.* Secaucus, NJ: Chartwell Books, 1992.

Cohen, Hennig and Tristram Potter Coffin, eds. *The Folklore of American Holidays.* Detroit, MI: Gale Research Company, 1987.

Coleman, William L. *Today's Handbook of Bible Times and Customs.* Minneapolis, MN: Bethany House Publishers, 1984.

Collins, Carolyn and Christina Eriksson. *The World of Little House.* New York: HarperCollins Publishers, 1996.

Cooke, Gillian, ed. *A Celebration of Christmas.* New York: G. P. Putnam's Sons, 1980.

Cowie, L.W. and Gummer, John Selwyn. *The Christian Calendar.* Springfield, MA: G & C Merriam Company, 1974.

Cross, F. L. and Livingstone, E.A. *Oxford Dictionary of the Christian*

Church. New York: Oxford University Press, 1997.

Douglas, George William. *American Book of Days*. H.W. Wilson Company, 1978, third edition.

Dues, Greg. *Catholic Customs and Traditions*. Mystic, CT: Twenty-third Publications, 1992.

Ferguson, George. Signs &Symbols in Christian Art. New York: Oxford University Press, 1954.

Foley, Daniel J. *Christmas the World Over*. Philadelphia, PA: Chilton Books, 1963.

Garrison, Webb. *A Treasury of Christmas Stories*. Nashville, TN: Rutledge Hill Press, 1990.

Hamilton, Edith. *Mythology*. Little, Brown, and Company, 1940.

Hartman, Rachel. *The Joys of Easter*. New York: Meredith Press, 1967.

Heaps, Willard A. *Birthstones*. New York: Meredith Press, 1969.

Hislop, Alexander. *The Two Babylons or The Papal Worship Proved to be the Worship of Nimrod and His Wife*. n.p.: n.d. Kindle edition.

Hole, Christina. *Christmas and Its Customs*. New York: M. Barrows and Company, 1958.

Hottes, Alfred C. *1001 Christmas Facts and Fancies*. New York: A.T. DeLa Mare Company, Inc., 1937.

Huber, Leonard V. *Mardi Gras: A Pictorial History of Carnival in New Orleans*. Gretna, LA: Pelican Publishing Co., 1977.

Hughes, Paul. *Days of the Week*. Ada, OK: Garrett Educational Corporation, 1989.

Ickis, Marguerite. *Book of Religious Holidays and Celebrations*. New York: Dodd, Mead and Company, 1966.

Johnson, Kevin Orlin. *Why Do Catholics Do That?* New York: Ballantine Books, 1994.

Kelley, Emily. *April Fools' Day*. Minneapolis, MN: Carolrhoda Books, 1983.

Kinser, Samuel. *Carnival, American Style: Mardi Gras at New Orleans and Mobile*. Chicago, IL: University of Chicago Press, 1990.

Krytle, Maymie R. *All About American Holidays*. New York: Harper & Brother Publishers, 1962.

Krytle, Maymie R. *All About Christmas*. New York: Harper & Brother Publishers, 1954.

Lankford, Mary D. *Christmas Around the World*. New York: Morrow Junior Books, 1995.

Lindahl, Carl, McNamara, John, and Lindow, John. *Medieval Folklore*. New York: Oxford University Press, 2002.

Livingstone, Sheila. *Scottish Festivals*. Edinburgh: Birlinn Limited, 1997.

Lord, Priscilla Sawyer. *Easter Garland*. Philadelphia, PA: Chilton Books, 1963.

Luther, Martin. *Against Catholicism*. n.p.: n.d. Kindle edition.

Luther, Martin. *The Babylonian Captivity of the Church*. n.p.: n.d. Kindle edition.

Maccullouch, J.A. *The Religion of the Ancient Celts*. n.p.: n.d. Kindle edition.

Maier, Paul L. *First Christmas: the True and Unfamiliar Story*. New York: Harper & Row, 1971.

Maier, Paul L. *First Easter: the True and Unfamiliar Story*. New York: Harper & Row, 1973.

Marsh, Dave and Steve Propes. *Merry Christmas, Baby: Holiday Music from Bing to Sting*. Boston, MA: Little, Brown, and Company, 1993.

Maclagan, Robert Craig. *Scottish Myths: Notes on Scottish History and Tradition*. n.p.: AlbaCraft Publishing, 2013. Kindle edition.

Miles, Clement A. *Christmas Customs and Traditions*. New York: Dover Publications, 1976.

Miller, Steve. *The Contemporary Christian Music Debate*. Wheaton, IL: Tyndale House Publishers, 1993.

Myers, Robert J. *Celebrations: the Complete Book of American Holidays*. Garden City, NY: Doubleday & Company, 1972.

Newall, Venetia. *An Egg at Easter*. Bloomington, IN: Indiana University Press, 1971.

O'Neal, Debbie Trafton. The *Advent Wreath*. Minneapolis, MN: Augsburg Publishing House, 1988.

Powell, Matthew. *The Christmas Crèche*. Boston, MA: Pauline Books and Media, 1997.

Restad, Penne. *Christmas in America*. New York: Oxford University Press, 1995.

Reynolds, William J. *Christ and the Carols*, Nashville, TN: Broadman Press, 1967.

Richards, Katharine Lambert. *How Christmas Came to the Sunday-Schools*. New York: Dodd, Mead, and Company, 1934.

Roberts, Timothy. *The Celts in Myth and Legend*. Michael Friedman Publishing Group: 1995.

Rordorf, Willy. *Sunday*, London: SCM Press Ltd, 1968.

Rosen, Ceil and Rosen, Moishe. *Christ in the Passover*. Chicago, IL: Moody Press, 1978.

Routley, Erik. *The English Carol*. New York: Oxford University Press, 1959.

Ryken, Leland. *Worldly Saints*. Grand Rapids, MI: Zondervan Publishing House, 1986.

Sanson, William. *A Book of Christmas*. New York: McGraw-Hill, 1968.

Schneider, Tammi J., *An Introduction to Ancient Mesopotamian Religion*. Grand Rapids, MI: Wm. B. Eerdmans Publishing Co., 2011. Kindle edition.

Schuman, Henry. *4000 Years of Christmas*. New York: Earl W. County, 1948.

Sinclair, Sir George. *Letters to the Protestants of Scotland*. Edinburgh: Jonestone and Hunter, n.d. Google electronic download.

Snyder, Phillip. *December 25th: the Joys of Christmas Past*. New York: Dodd, Mead, & Company, 1985.

Strassfeld, Michael. *The Jewish Holidays*. New York: Harper & Row, 1985.

Steingroot, Ira. *Keeping Passover*. New York: HarperCollins, 1995.

Stevens, Patricia Bunning. *Merry Christmas: A History of the Holiday*. New York: Macmillan Publishing Co., 1979.

Teringo, J. Robert. *The Land and People Jesus Knew*. Minneapolis, MN: Bethany House Publishers, 1985.

Thompson, J. A. *Handbook of Life in Bible Times*. Downers Grove, IL: Inter-Varsity Press, 1986.

Thorpe, Peter James and Nick. *Ancient Mysteries*. New York: Ballantine Books, 1999.

Tuleja, Tad. *Curious Customs*. New York: Harmony Books, 1987.

Vander Laan, Ray. *Echoes of His Presence*. Colorado Springs, CO: Focus on the Family, 1996.

Weinstein-Farson, Laurie. *The Wampanoag*. New York: Chelsea House Publishers, 1989.

Weiser, Francis X. *The Christmas Book*. New York: Harcourt, Brace & Company, 1952.

Weiser, Francis X. *The Easter Book*. New York: Harcourt, Brace and Company, Inc., 1954.

Weiser, Francis X. *Handbook of Christian Feasts and Customs.* New York: Harcourt, Brace & World, Inc., 1952.

Weiser, Francis X. *The Holyday Book.* London: Staples Press Limited.

Whittemore, Carroll E. ed. *Symbols of the Church.* Abingdon Press, 1959.

Wight, Fred H. *Manners and Customs of Bible Lands.* Chicago, IL: Moody Press, 1953.

Wilcox, David. *Carols for Christmas.* New York: The Metropolitan Museum of Art and Holt, Rinehart and Winston, 1983.

Wilder, Laura Ingalls. *Little House on the Prairie.* New York: Harper & Row, 1935.

Wilder, Laura Ingalls. *On the Banks of Plum Creek.* New York: Harper & Row, 1937.

Wilson, Jan. *Feasting for Festivals.* Batavia, IL: Lion Publishing, 1990.

Wilson, Patricia Dreame, ed. *American Country Christmas 1990.* Alabama: Oxmoor House, 1990.

Woodrow, Ralph. *The Babylon Connection?.* Palm Springs, CA: Ralph Woodrow Evangelistic Association, Inc., 2004.

Woodrow, Ralph. *Christmas Reconsidered.* Palm Springs, CA: Ralph Woodrow Evangelistic Association, Inc., 2006.

Woodrow, Ralph. *Easter, Is it Pagan?.* Palm Springs, CA: Ralph Woodrow Evangelistic Association, Inc., 1998.

www.biblestudytools.com

www.bobscandies.com

Zimmerman, Martha. *Celebrating the Christian Year.* Minneapolis, MN: Bethany House Publishers, 1994.

ABOUT THE AUTHOR

Susan E. Richardson makes her home in Clinton, MS. She has managed Christian bookstores in Mississippi and Texas, and now writes and offers freelance critique services. When not at the computer, she enjoys gardening and photography. She has a passion for meeting people's needs through the written word and wrote this book in response to many customer requests for information about American holidays during her days in Christian retail. To see more of her work, check out her website at www.chewedpetunias.com

26688006R00107

Made in the USA
Lexington, KY
11 October 2013